JOSEPHINE LONG

Super Easy Teen Cookbook

101 Detailed Full-Color Delicious Recipes

WITH STEP-BY-STEP VISUALS & ESSENTIAL FACTS

TABLE OF CONTENTS

01 BREAKFAST

02 LUNCH

TABLE OF CONTENTS

03 DINNER

04 DESSERTS

How to Use Your Cookbook?

Cheers from the world of American cuisine! You will learn how to prepare delectable dishes and become an expert chef with the help of this cookbook. Let's investigate how to get the most out of this culinary journey!

Off to a Good Start

Scroll through the Table of Contents to find what you're searching for. It is divided into parts that are easy to read and explore. Are you looking for a certain dish? Select the appropriate page!

Make Wise Meal Plans

For daily inspiration, check out the meal plan section. Each day links directly to a recipe, making meal preparation easier and keeping you organized for the entire month.

Make Healthier Choices

Our recipes frequently call for healthier substitutions for ingredients while maintaining the delicious flavors. It all comes down to enjoying your favorite foods and boosting their nutritional value!

Awareness about Nutrition

Discover the nutritional advantages of the ingredients you use. You may utilize this information to make well-informed decisions regarding your nutrition and general health.

Modifying Portions

If a recipe calls for six servings but needs only four, cut the ingredients by a third. Increase the ingredients accordingly for bigger gatherings to make sure everyone gets a taste!

Efficiency in the Kitchen

Prepare ahead to speed up the cooking process, chop veggies, measure seasonings, and make sauces in advance. Read the Ingredient Section and prepare to start cooking. As you cook, wipe off surfaces and utensils to keep your workspace neat. This will clear up clutter and improve your kitchen experience.

Essential Utensils for the Kitchen

- ***Knives with shapes*** are ideal for precisely dicing and slicing.
- ***Kitchen scales*** are necessary for precise ingredient measurement.
- **Cutting boards:** Using different cutting boards (one for veggies, one for meats) can keep your prep work organized and prevent cross-contamination.
- ***Measuring cups and spoons:*** These are essential for precisely measuring liquid and dry materials in baking and cooking.
- ***Mixing Bowls:*** A set of mixing bowls in different sizes is necessary when preparing and mixing components.

- **Silicone spatulas:** These pliable implements are excellent for removing any remaining batter or sauce from your dishes and pans, and they are resistant to melting even at elevated temperatures.
- **Whisks:** Whisks are available in a variety of sizes and forms to suit the work at hand, and they are essential for beating eggs and mixing sauces.
- **Peeler:** A quality peeler allows for smoother and faster peeling, which can save you time while preparing fruits and vegetables.
- **Grater:** You can shred cheese, veggies, and even citrus fruits with a multi-sided grater.
- **Cooking thermometer:** A cooking thermometer guarantees that meats and other foods are cooked to the proper doneness and safety.
- ***Tongs:*** An extension of your hands in the kitchen, tongs are useful for rotating, flipping, and serving food.
- ***Colander*** is perfect for washing fruits and vegetables as well as draining pasta.
- ***Blenders and food processors*** are excellent kitchen tools for rapidly chopping, blending, and creating sauces and smoothies.

Explore New Tastes

Be bold and modify recipes with ingredients you prefer or have on hand. This may result in intriguing and unique flavor combinations.

Discover the craft of seasoning. Flavors can be greatly enhanced by adding herbs and spices at different stages of cooking. For example, adding fresh herbs toward the end of cooking helps to retain their flavor and aroma.

Use Fresh Ingredients

Use fresh meats, veggies, and herbs whenever possible. Your dishes will taste better and have more excellent textures when made with fresh ingredients.

The Advantages of Home Cooking

- ***Better Options:*** Home cooking is healthier than fast food because you can completely control what goes into it.
- ***Save Money:*** Generally, it costs less than going out to eat.
- **Spending Quality Time** with family and friends is a great way to bond.
- ***Developing Your Cooking Skills:*** Try new recipes to improve your cooking abilities.
- ***Impress Your Circle***: Picture yourself preparing a cooked supper for your loved ones. Cooking is a method of showing someone you care and wowing them, not only of feeding yourself.

Try International Cuisine

If your cookbook recipes call for using foreign ingredients, do so! Learning to cook food from many countries is a great way to broaden your horizons and learn about international cooking customs.

Food Presentation

Try several plate methods to create eye-catching visuals for your food. Even simple dishes can feel extraordinary and impress with their presentation.

Digital Tools

Use Cooking applications! Many applications have timers, substitutions, and conversion features. These tools make it simpler to follow and modify recipes correctly.

Ecological Methods

Cut Down on Food Wastage! Make meal plans that use leftovers creatively. For instance, stale bread can be made into croutons, and leftover veggies can be used in stews. Try to purchase produce that is grown nearby. It helps the local economy, tastes better, and is typically fresher.

Record Your Culinary Adventures:

Keep a notebook of the recipes you've tested, including any modifications you made and your views on each dish's pros and cons! This cookbook will come in handy as your culinary abilities grow. Using these extra pointers will improve your culinary skills and give you a deeper, more fulfilling cooking experience. Always keep in mind that each meal you prepare is a step toward developing your cooking skills and confidence.

Safe Cooking Techniques

1. **Never Leave Cooking Unattended:** When cooking, especially on high heat or with oils and fats, you should always remain in the kitchen. One of the main causes of kitchen fires is unattended cooking.
2. **Use Pot Holders and Oven Mitts:** When handling hot pans, baking trays, or pots, use oven mitts to prevent burns to your hands.
3. **Maintain a Fire Extinguisher** close by, making sure a fire extinguisher appropriate for kitchen fires is easily accessible. Learn how to use it so that you will be prepared for anything.
4. **Avoid Overloading Electrical Outlets**: To avoid electrical overloads, which can result in fires, only plug one high-wattage equipment into each outlet.
5. **Always Remember to Turn Off Appliances After Use**: After using burners, ovens, and other appliances, be sure they are turned off right away.
6. **To prevent spillage**, always watch what you're cooking and make sure the handles of your pots and pans are facing inward.
7. Use caution when **handling electric equipment**; ensure your hands are dry and keep cords away from hot surfaces.
8. **Maintain a Clean Cooking Area**: Clean up spills and clear the area of clutter. Food particles and built-up grease can ignite quickly.
9. **Secure Loose Clothes**: Dress appropriately for cooking. Steer clear of hanging clothes or loose sleeves that could catch fire or get caught in appliances.
10. **Use Appropriate Lighting**: Make sure the area where you are cooking is well-lit so you can see what you are doing clearly and the chance of an accident is decreased.
11. **Cool Hot Liquids Carefully**: Use caution to prevent spillage when working with hot liquids. To lessen the chance of scorching, wait until the water in a pot is manageable before moving it.

Have fun on your culinary journey!

MEAL PLANNER

	BREAKFAST	LUNCH	DINNER	DESSERT
1	Banana Bread (p. 26)	Submarine Sandwich (p. 67)	Lasagna (p. 72)	Ice Cream Sundae (p. 101)
2	Bacon, Egg, and Cheese Biscuit (p. 35)	Veggie Burger (p. 54)	Chicken Alfredo (p. 83)	Cheesecake (p. 105)
3	Croissants with Banana and Chocolate (p. 34)	Nachos (p. 65)	Chicken Parmesan (p. 70)	Banana Split (p. 109)
4	French Toast (p. 13)	Philly Cheesesteak (p. 57)	Fajitas (p. 74)	Rice Krispies Treats (p. 108)
5	Vegetable Casserole (p. 36)	Gyro (p. 68)	Spaghetti and Meatballs (p. 78)	Chocolate Cake (p. 106)
6	Bagels with Cream Cheese and Salmon (p. 16)	Cheeseburger (p. 42)	Classic Pizza (p. 71)	Brownies (p. 100)
7	Quick Oatmeal (p. 14)	Fish Tacos (p. 66)	Chicken and Dumplings (p. 94)	Donuts (p. 107)
8	Fruit Salad (p. 31)	Club Sandwich (p. 63)	Shepherd's Pie (p. 87)	Apple Pie (p. 104)
9	Breakfast Tacos (p. 21)	Cheese Quesadilla (p. 47)	Teriyaki Chicken (p. 85)	Cupcakes (p. 102)
10	Fried Eggs with Turkey or Chicken Sausage (p. 15)	Hot Dog (p. 60)	Chicken Pot Pie (p. 86)	Chocolate Chip Cookies (p. 103)
11	Fluffy Sweet Pancakes (p. 22)	Chicken Salad (p. 61)	Sloppy Joe Casserole (p. 95)	Chocolate Cake (p. 106)
12	Yogurt Parfait (p. 17)	Pasta Salad (p. 55)	Chicken Tacos (p. 79)	Cupcakes (p. 102)
13	Smoothie Bowl (p. 20)	Chicken Caesar Wrap (p. 51)	Oven-Baked Ribs (p. 73)	Ice Cream Sundae (p. 101)
14	Scrambled Egg (p. 12)	Turkey Sandwich (p. 44)	Baked Ziti (p. 80)	Rice Krispies Treats (p. 108)
15	Granola Bar (p. 29)	Basic Sushi Roll (p. 49)	Jambalaya (p. 89)	Chocolate Chip Cookies (p. 103)

BREAKFAST	LUNCH	DINNER	DESSERT	
Cereal with Milk (p. 28)	Grilled Cheese Sandwich (p. 40)	Chili (p. 88)	Cheesecake (p. 105)	16
Ricotta Pancakes (p. 18)	Chicken Tenders (p. 56)	Roast Chicken (p. 82)	Apple Pie (p. 104)	17
Breakfast Sandwich (p. 10)	Spaghetti with Marinara Sauce (p. 50)	Enchiladas (p. 81)	Banana Split (p. 109)	18
Hash Browns (p. 23)	Caprese Sandwich (p. 69)	Beef Stroganoff (p. 75)	Donuts (p. 107)	19
Banana Oatmeal Muffins (p. 24)	Pita Pocket with Hummus and Veggies (p. 58)	Fried Chicken (p. 77)	Brownies (p. 100)	20
Eggs Benedict Sandwich (p. 25)	Personal Pan Pizza (p. 64)	BBQ Pulled Pork (p. 91)	Apple Pie (p. 104)	21
Breakfast Salad (p. 38)	Tacos (p. 43)	Stuffed Bell Peppers (p. 92)	Chocolate Cake (p. 106)	22
Classic Blueberry Muffins (p. 33)	Macaroni and Cheese (p. 48)	Shrimp Scampi (p. 76)	Banana Split (p. 109)	23
Pancake (p. 11)	Chicken Nuggets (p. 41)	Goulash (p. 96)	Cupcakes (p. 102)	24
Sausage Rolls (p. 27)	Caesar Salad (p. 45)	Baked Salmon (p. 93)	Ice Cream Sundae (p. 101)	25
Cinnabon rolls (p. 30)	Pulled Pork Sandwich (p. 53)	Pork Chops (p. 84)	Cheesecake (p. 105)	26
Crepes (p. 37)	Tuna Salad Sandwich (p. 59)	Stir Fry (p. 97)	Chocolate Chip Cookies (p. 103)	27
Avocado Toast (p. 19)	BLT Sandwich (p. 46)	Chicken Curry (p. 90)	Brownies (p. 100)	28
Breakfast Burritos (p. 32)	Sloppy Joes (p. 62)	Meatloaf (p. 98)	Donuts (p. 107)	29
Boiled Egg (p. 19)	Meatball Sandwich (p. 52)	Baked Ham (p. 99)	Rice Krispies Treats (p. 108)	30

Breakfast
Boiled Egg

PREP 0 MIN

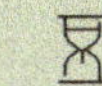
COOK 4-10 MIN

1 EGG = 1 SERVE

Benefits of boiled eggs

Rich in vitamins B,D,E,and A

To help fight off germs

Rich in omega-3 fatty acids

For brainpower

6 grams of protein in one egg

To have healthy skin, hair, and nails.

To grow muscles

Low in calories (70-80) calories

To stay fit

Ingredients & Tools

- Eggs (as many as you want to cook)
- Pot large enough to hold all eggs in a single layer
- Timer (or a smartphone with a timer app)
- Slotted spoon or tablespoon
- Bowl with ice water (for cooling down the eggs quickly if eating right away or storing)

Tips for Success:

- Adding a Pinch of Salt: Some people find that adding a pinch of salt to the boiling water makes peeling the eggs easier.
- Cutting boiled eggs in half and adding a bit of salt or spices can enhance their flavor.

It is recommended to eat no more than 3 eggs per day.
Overall, boiling eggs is often considered one of the healthiest ways to prepare them.

METHOD

Step 1: Prep the Eggs
Place your eggs in a single layer at the bottom of the pot. Avoid stacking them to ensure they cook evenly.
Fill the pot with enough water to cover the eggs by about an inch.

Step 2: Heat Things Up
Put the pot on the stove and turn the heat to high. Wait for the water to come to a full, rolling boil.

Step 3: Once the water is boiling, set your timer based on how you like your eggs:

- Soft-boiled eggs: 4-5 minutes for a runny yolk and firm white.
- Medium-boiled eggs: 6-7 minutes for a partially set yolk and firm white.
- Hard-boiled eggs: 8-10 minutes for fully cooked yolks and whites.

Step 4: Cool Down
As soon as your timer goes off, use the slotted spoon to remove the eggs from the hot water and transfer them to the bowl of ice water. Let them cool for a couple of minutes. This stops the cooking process and makes the eggs easier to handle and peel.

Step 5: Peel and Enjoy!
Tap the egg on a hard surface to crack the shell, then gently peel it off under running cold water (this helps get the shell off cleanly). Your boiled eggs are ready to eat!

Per Serving:

- **Calories:** 70
- **Total Carbohydrates:** Less than 1 gram
- **Protein:** About 6 grams

Fat: 5 grams
Sugar: 0 grams
Fiber: 0 grams

NOTES

RATING

DIFFICULTY

Breakfast Sandwich

PREP 0 MIN | COOK 20 MIN | 1 SERVE

Benefits of Breakfast Sandwich

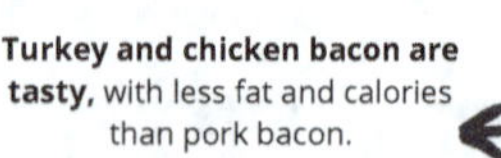

Turkey and chicken bacon are tasty, with less fat and calories than pork bacon.

Tomato: Rich in vitamin C and antioxidants.

To help fight off germs

Avocado: Contains healthy fats.

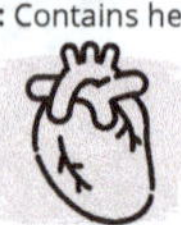

To have a strong heart ready to run a maraphon

Whole Grain Bun or English Muffin provides fiber and complex carbohydrates.

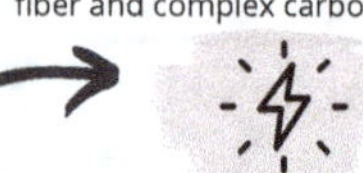

To energize you

Eggs are high in protein, vitamin B12, and choline.

To stay smart

Reduced-Fat Cheese provides calcium and protein

For strong bones and teeth

Ingredients & Tools

- 1 whole grain English muffin or whole wheat burger bun
- 2 large eggs
- 2 slices of turkey or chicken bacon
- 2 slices of tomato
- 2 slices of avocado
- 2 lettuce leaves
- 1 slice of reduced-fat cheese
- Salt and pepper, to taste
- Pan
- Spatula
- Knife

Tips for Success:

- Customize the sandwich with additional toppings like spinach, bell peppers, or onions.
- Cook the eggs according to your preference, but avoid overcooking to retain their nutritional value.

It is recommended to choose whole grain bread instead of the white kinds to help your body run better and not gain extra weight. Limit your daily bread consumption to ensure you're not overloading on simple carbohydrates, which can contribute to weight gain and fluctuations in blood sugar levels.

METHOD

Step 1: Cook the turkey or chicken bacon in a skillet over medium heat until crispy. Remove from skillet and set aside.

Step 2: Cook Eggs: In the same skillet, add olive oil or butter. Crack the eggs gently to avoid breaking the yolks into the skillet and cook them to your desired doneness (over-easy -2-3 minutes, or over-medium, over-hard- 3-4 minutes).

Step 3: Toast the English muffin or whole wheat burger bun in a toaster or a separate skillet. If you're using a toaster, simply place the English muffin halves in the toaster slots and toast them until lightly browned. If you're using a skillet, you can toast the English muffin halves in the skillet over medium heat, flipping them occasionally until they are lightly browned on both sides.

Step 4: On one half of the English muffin, layer a slice of cheese, a slice of tomato, a slice of avocado, two slices of bacon, and the cooked eggs. Season with salt and pepper, if desired. Close the sandwich with the other half of the English muffin. Serve the breakfast sandwich hot and enjoy!

Per Serving:

- **Calories:** 500-550 kcal
- **Total Carbohydrates:** 35-40 grams
- **Dietary Fiber:** 8-10 grams
- **Sugars:** 5-7 grams
- **Protein:** 30-35 grams
- **Total Fat:** 25-30 grams
- **Cholesterol:** 370-400 mg
- **Sodium:** 600-800 mg

NOTES

RATING

DIFFICULTY

Pancake

PREP 5 MIN

COOK 15 MIN

4 SERVE

Benefits of Panckakes

Ingredients & Tools

- 1 cup all-purpose flour (or whole wheat for a healthier option)
- 2 tablespoons sugar (can substitute with honey or maple syrup)
- 1 tablespoon baking powder
- 1/4 teaspoon salt
- 1 cup milk (use almond or oat milk for a dairy-free version)
- 1 egg
- 2 tablespoons melted butter or vegetable oil
- Optional: 1/2 cup of blueberries or chocolate chips
- A pan
- Ladle and spatula

Tips for Success:

- **Make It a Meal:** Add a scoop of Greek yogurt or a handful of nuts for extra protein.
- **Get Creative:** Customize your pancakes with different mix-ins or toppings like banana slices, diced apple, or a sprinkle of cinnamon.

It is recommended to choose whole wheat flour instead of the white kinds to help your body run better and not gain extra weight. Limit your daily flour consumption to ensure you're not overloading on simple carbohydrates, which can contribute to weight gain and fluctuations in blood sugar levels.

METHOD

Step 1: Mix Dry Ingredients: In a large bowl, combine the flour, sugar, baking powder, and salt. Stir well to mix.

Step 2: In another bowl, whisk together the milk, egg, and melted butter or oil. Pour this mixture into the dry ingredients, stirring just until combined. If adding blueberries or chocolate chips, fold them in gently.

Step 3: Heat a non-stick skillet or griddle over medium heat. You can test if it's ready by sprinkling a few drops of water on it; if they dance and sizzle, it's ready.

Step 4: Pour about 1/4 cup of batter for each pancake onto the skillet. Cook until bubbles form on the surface and the edges look set, about 2-3 minutes. Flip and cook the other side until golden brown, about 2 more minutes.

Step 5: Serve the pancakes hot with your favorite toppings like fresh fruit, yogurt, or a drizzle of honey.

Per Serving:

- **Calories:** 250-280 calories
- **Total Carbohydrates:** 32-36 grams
- **Dietary Fiber:** 1-2 grams
- **Sugars:** 8-10 grams

Protein: 6-7 grams
Total Fat: 11-13 grams
Cholesterol: 50-55 mg
Sodium: 400-450 mg

NOTES

RATING

DIFFICULTY

Scrambled Egg

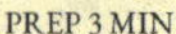

PREP 3 MIN COOK 3 MIN 1 SERVE

Benefits of Scrumbled Egg

Eggs are rich in vitamins B12,E, D and A

for strong bones and teeth

Rich in choline

To stay smart

Contain lutein and zeaxanthin, antioxidants

For Eye Health

6 grams of **protein** in one egg

To have healthy skin, hair, and nails.

To grow muscles

Ingredients & Tools

- 2 eggs
- 1 tablespoon butter or cooking oil
- Salt and pepper, to taste

Optional: shredded cheese, diced vegetables, cooked bacon or ham

- Pan
- Spatula

Tips for Success:

Use Low to Medium Heat: Cooking scrambled eggs over low to medium heat allows them to cook gently and evenly without becoming tough or rubbery.

Don't Overbeat the Eggs: Avoid overbeating the eggs, as this can lead to a tough and dense texture. Simply whisk them until the yolks and whites are just combined.

It is recommended to eat no more than 3 eggs per day. Use minimal cooking oil when preparing scrambled eggs.

METHOD

Step 1: Crack Eggs: Crack the eggs into a bowl and beat them with a fork until well mixed. Season with salt and pepper.

Tip: Use Fresh Eggs

Step 2: Heat Pan: Place a non-stick skillet over medium heat and add the butter or cooking oil. Let it melt and coat the pan.

Step 3: Cook Eggs: Pour the beaten eggs into the skillet. Let them cook undisturbed for a few seconds until the edges start to set.

Step 4: Scramble: Using a spatula, gently push the eggs from the edges towards the center, allowing the uncooked eggs to flow to the edges. Continue this process until the eggs are mostly cooked but still slightly runny.

Step 6: Serve: Remove the skillet from the heat and transfer the scrambled eggs to a plate. Serve hot and enjoy!

Step 5: Add Extras (Optional): If desired, add shredded cheese, diced vegetables, or cooked bacon or ham to the eggs and continue to cook until the cheese is melted and the vegetables are heated through.

Per Serving:

- **Calories:** Approximately 200-220
- **Total Carbohydrates:** 1-2 grams
- **Protein:** 12-14 grams
- **Fat:** 14-16 grams
- **Sugar:** 0 grams
- **Fiber:** 0 grams
- **Cholesterol:** 370-390 mg

NOTES

RATING

DIFFICULTY

French Toast

PREP 5 MIN

COOK 15 MIN

4 SERVE

Benefits of French Toast

Using **whole wheat bread** instead of all-purpose flour

Will be beneficial for digestive health

12 grams of **protein** in a serving

To grow muscles

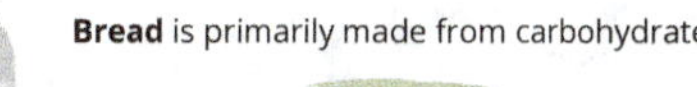

Bread is primarily made from carbohydrates

To quickly energize you

Milk in pancakes - source of calcium

For strong bones and teeth

Ingredients & Tools

- 8 slices of whole grain bread (for added fiber)
- 4 eggs
- 1 cup milk (can use almond, soy, or oat milk for a dairy-free option)
- 2 tablespoons sugar (optional, can substitute with honey or maple syrup)
- 1 teaspoon vanilla extract
- 1/2 teaspoon ground cinnamon
- Butter or non-stick cooking spray for the pan
- Optional toppings: fresh berries, sliced bananas, a sprinkle of powdered sugar, or a drizzle of maple syrup
- Pan
- Spatula

Tips for Success

Thicker slices work best for French toast. Brioche, challah, or any thick-cut white bread are excellent choices because they are soft and will absorb the egg mixture well without falling apart. French toast is a great way to use up bread that's starting to go stale.

It is recommended to choose whole grain bread instead of the white kinds to help your body run better and not gain extra weight. Limit your daily bread consumption to ensure you're not overloading on simple carbohydrates, which can contribute to weight gain and fluctuations in blood sugar levels.

METHOD

Step 1: In a medium bowl, whisk together the eggs, milk, sugar, vanilla extract, and cinnamon with a whisker or a fork until well blended.

Step 2: Dip each slice of bread into the egg mixture, allowing it to soak for a few seconds on each side. Make sure each piece is well-coated.

Step 3: Heat a large skillet or griddle over medium heat and add butter or spray with non-stick cooking spray. Place the soaked bread slices in the skillet, cooking until golden brown on both sides, about 2-3 minutes per side.

Step 4: Serve the French toast hot with your chosen toppings.

Pair your French toast with a protein source like Greek yogurt or a handful of nuts. Try different spices like nutmeg or cardamom in the egg mixture, or add orange zest for a fresh twist.

Per Serving:

- **Calories:** 250-300 calories
- **Total Carbohydrates:** 30-35 grams
- **Dietary Fiber:** 4-5 grams
- **Sugars:** 8-10 grams
- **Protein:** 12-14 grams
- **Total Fat:** 9-11 grams
- **Cholesterol:** 170-190 mg
- **Sodium:** 200-250 mg

NOTES

RATING

DIFFICULTY

Quick Oatmeal

PREP 5 MIN | COOK 0 MIN | 1 SERVE

Benefits of Oatmeal

Ingredients & Tools

- 1/2 cup instant oats
- 1 cup water or milk (use almond, soy, or oat milk for extra nutrients)
- Pinch of salt
- Optional: 1 tablespoon of honey or maple syrup for sweetness
- Optional toppings: fresh fruit (like berries or banana slices), nuts, seeds (like chia or flaxseed), a spoonful of peanut butter, or a sprinkle of cinnamon

Tips for Success

- **Balanced Breakfast:** Pair your French toast with a protein source like Greek yogurt or a handful of nuts to balance the meal and keep you fuller longer.
- **Experiment with Flavors:** Try different spices like nutmeg or cardamom in the egg mixture, or add orange zest for a fresh twist.
- **Use Leftovers:** French toast is a great way to use up bread that's starting to go stale.

It is recommended to use the steaming or microwave method without using a stove because it is an excellent choice for those who value speed and simplicity in cooking. This method also preserves more nutrients than some other oatmeal cooking methods.

METHOD

Step 1: In a microwave-safe bowl, combine the oats and a pinch of salt with water or milk. Stir to mix.

Step 2: Microwave on high for about 2-3 minutes. Keep an eye on the bowl to prevent the oatmeal from boiling over.

if you don't have a microwave use steaming method: Cover the bowl tightly with a lid or plate and let the oatmeal sit for 3-5 minutes to allow it to steep and become soft.

Step 3: Add Flavors and Toppings: Remove the bowl from the microwave, stir in any sweeteners like honey or maple syrup if using. Top with your favorite toppings like fruits, nuts, or seeds for added flavor and nutrients.

Step 4: Serve: Enjoy your warm and comforting bowl of instant oatmeal.

Per Serving:

- **Calories:** 100-150 calories
- **Total Carbohydrates:** 19-27 grams
- **Dietary Fiber:** 3-4 grams
- **Sugars:** 0-1 grams
- **Protein:** 3-5 grams
- **Total Fat:** 1-3 grams
- **Cholesterol:** 0 mg
- **Sodium:** 75-200 mg

NOTES

RATING

DIFFICULTY

Fried Eggs with Turkey or Chicken Sausage

Ingredients & Tools

- 2 eggs
- 2 turkey or chicken sausage links
- 1 tablespoon olive oil or butter
- Salt and pepper, to taste
- Pan
- Spatula
- Optional: sliced avocado, tomatoes, whole grain toast

Tips for Success:

Eggs are best served hot and fresh. Serve the dish immediately after cooking for the best flavor and texture.

When choosing the right sausages opting for sausages made from lean meats like turkey or chicken instead of pork or beef.

It is recommended to look for sausages that contain mostly meat with few additives. The shorter the list of ingredients, the better. Try to find sausages labeled as "low sodium" or check the nutritional information to choose options with less salt.

METHOD

Step 1: Cut the sausages in half or into smaller pieces, if desired.

Step 2: Preheat the skillet over medium heat before adding the olive oil or butter. This helps prevent sticking and ensures even cooking. Add the sausage pieces and cook them according to the package instructions until they are browned and cooked. Make sure to cook the sausage thoroughly until it's no longer pink in the middle. Remove the sausages from the skillet and set them aside.

Step 3: In the same skillet, add olive oil or butter. Crack the eggs gently to avoid breaking the yolks into the skillet and cook them to your desired doneness (over-easy -2-3 minutes, or over-medium, over-hard- 3-4 minutes).

Step 4: Use a spatula to carefully flip the eggs if you're cooking them over-easy or over-medium. Season the eggs with salt and pepper.

Step 5: Serve the fried eggs with the cooked sausage links. Add optional sliced avocado, tomatoes, and whole-grain toast on the side if desired.

Per Serving:

- **Calories:** Approximately 250-300 calories
- **Total Carbohydrates:** 1-3 grams
- **Protein:** 18-22 grams
- **Total Fat:** 18-22 grams
- **Cholesterol:** 185-215 mg
- **Sugar:** 0-1 grams
- **Fiber:** 0 grams

NOTES

RATING

DIFFICULTY

Bagels with Cream Cheese and Salmon

PREP 10 MIN

COOK 0 MIN

2 SERVE

Benefits of Bagels with Cream Cheese and Salmon

Vegetables add vitamins and fiber

to keep your bones, skin, and eyes healthy.

Salmon provides omega-3 fatty acids and protein

to help fight off germs

Bagels are a good source of complex carbohydrates

to quickly energize you

Choose **whole grain bagels** to increase your fiber intake and help lower cholesterol levels.

Promote heart health.

For regular bowel movements and prevents constipation.

Ingredients & Tools

- 2 bagels (choose whole grain for more fiber)
- 4 tablespoons cream cheese (opt for low-fat or flavored varieties like strawberry or garden vegetable)
- Optional fillings:
- Sliced cucumbers
- Tomato slices
- Red onion rings
- Capers
- Smoked salmon (for a luxurious treat)
- Sliced avocado

It is recommended to choose whole grain bread instead of the white kinds to help your body run better and not gain extra weight. Limit your daily bread consumption to ensure you're not overloading on simple carbohydrates, which can contribute to weight gain and fluctuations in blood sugar levels.

Tips for Success

- **Creative Combinations:** Experiment with different cream cheese flavors and toppings to find your favorite combination. Try making a sweet version with almond butter and banana slices.
- **Take with you to school:** This meal is quick to prepare, making it perfect for a busy morning or a hearty snack.

METHOD

Step 1: Prepare the Bagels: Cut each bagel in half horizontally using a serrated knife. Be sure to keep your fingers away from the blade as you slice through the bagel with a sawing motion.

Step 2: Toast the Bagels: Toast the bagel halves in a toaster or under a broiler until they are golden and crispy. This adds texture and flavor.

Step 3: Spread each half generously with cream cheese. The warmth of the toasted bagel will make the cream cheese easier to spread.

Step 4: Layer your chosen fillings on one half of each bagel. Whether it's crisp cucumber, smoky salmon, or creamy avocado, these add taste, texture, and nutritional value. Place the other half of the bagel on top, press down gently, and serve.

Per Serving:

- **Calories:** 400-450 calories
- **Protein:** 15-20 grams
- **Carbohydrates**: 45-50 grams
- **Dietary Fiber**: 6-8 grams
- **Fat:** 15-20 grams
- **Saturated Fat:** Varies depending on the cream cheese choice
- **Cholesterol:** Varies depending on cream cheese choice and smoked salmon
- **Sodium:** Varies depending on cream cheese variety, capers, and smoked salmon

NOTES

RATING

DIFFICULTY

Yogurt Parfait

PREP 10 MIN | COOK 0 MIN | 1 SERVE

Benefits of Yogurt Parfait

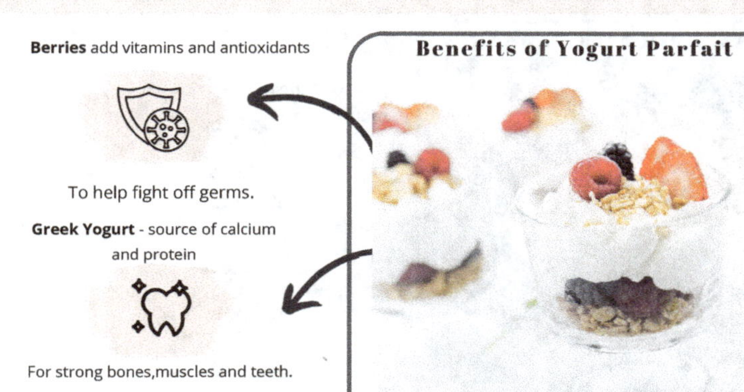

Berries add vitamins and antioxidants

To help fight off germs.

Greek Yogurt - source of calcium and protein

For strong bones,muscles and teeth.

Granola is a good source of complex carbohydrates

To quickly energize you.

Yogurt contains probiotics that help in maintaining a healthy gut microbiota.

for regular bowel movements and prevents constipation.

Ingredients & Tools

- 1 cup plain Greek yogurt
- 1/2 cup granola
- 1/2 cup mixed berries (such as strawberries, blueberries, and raspberries)
- 1 tablespoon honey (optional)

Tips for Success

Customization: Choose different types of fruits or granola. Try using seasonal fruits or different flavored yogurts to mix things up. Consider adding nuts, seeds, or a sprinkle of cinnamon. Nuts and seeds add healthy fats and additional protein, while cinnamon can add flavor without extra sugar.

It is recommended to incorporate yogurt into your diet several times a week, as it can help you take full advantage of its health benefits, including probiotics for gut health and calcium for bones.

METHOD

Step 1: In a glass or bowl, start with a layer of Greek yogurt. Add a layer of granola on top of the yogurt.

Step 2: Next, add a layer of mixed berries. Repeat the layering process until the glass is filled.

Step 3: Next, add a layer of mixed berries. Drizzle honey over the top for added sweetness, if desired. Serve immediately or refrigerate until ready to eat.

Per Serving:

- **Calories:** 350 kcal
- **Protein:** 20 g
- **Fat:** 8 g
- **Carbohydrates:** 50 g
- **Fiber:** 5 g
- **Sugar:** 30 g (includes natural and added sugars)

NOTES

RATING

DIFFICULTY

Ricotta Pancakes

PREP 10 MIN

COOK 15 MIN

8 SERVES

Benefits of Ricotta Pancakes

The carbohydrates in the **flour and sugar**

To quickly energize you.

Milk and ricotta cheese in pancakes - source of calcium

For strong bones and teeth.

Ricotta cheese is rich in protein

To have healthy skin, hair, and nails.

To grow muscles.

Ingredients & Tools

- 1 cup all-purpose flour
- 2 tablespoons granulated sugar
- 1/2 teaspoon baking powder
- 1/4 teaspoon salt
- 3/4 cup ricotta cheese
- 2 large eggs
- 1/2 cup milk
- 1 teaspoon vanilla extract
- Butter or oil, for cooking
- Optional: fresh berries, maple syrup, or powdered sugar for serving

Tips for Success:

- Use Fresh Ingredients: Make sure your ricotta cheese, eggs, and other ingredients are fresh for the best flavor and texture.
- Don't Overmix the Batter: When combining the wet and dry ingredients, mix just until everything is incorporated. Overmixing can make the pancakes dense instead of light and fluffy.

Ricotta pancakes are versatile and can be enjoyed at any time of day. Experiment with different toppings and sides to find your perfect combination.

METHOD

Step 1: In a large mixing bowl, whisk together the flour, sugar, baking powder, and salt.

Step 2: In another bowl, combine the ricotta cheese, eggs, milk, and vanilla extract. Mix well until smooth.

Step 3: Fold the ricotta mixture into the dry ingredients, stirring until just combined. Be careful not to overmix to keep the pancakes fluffy.

Step 4: Heat a non-stick skillet over medium heat and brush with a little butter or oil.

Step 5: Pour 1/4 cup of batter for each pancake onto the skillet. Cook until bubbles form on the surface and the edges look set, about 2-3 minutes.

Step 6: Flip the pancakes and cook for another 2 minutes or until golden brown and cooked through. Serve hot with your choice of toppings like fresh berries, maple syrup, or a sprinkle of powdered sugar.

Per Serving:

- **Calories:** 140 kcal
- **Protein:** 6 g
- **Fat:** 6 g
- **Carbohydrates:** 16 g
- **Fiber:** 0.5 g
- **Sugar:** 4 g

NOTES

RATING

DIFFICULTY

Avocado Toast

PREP 10 MIN

COOK 0 MIN

1 SERVING

Benefits of avocado toast

Avocados are high in monounsaturated fats

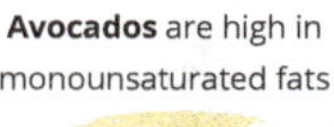

promote heart health

Whole grain bread and avocado

aids in digestion and promotes gut health.

Avocado is a superfood. It contains vitamins C, E, K, and B-6, as well as riboflavin, niacin, folate, pantothenic acid, magnesium, and potassium.

To have healthy skin, hair, and nails.

Will help fight inflammation and support immune health.

To grow muscles.

Ingredients & Tools

- 1 ripe avocado
- 2 slices of whole-grain bread
- 1 tablespoon olive oil
- Salt, to taste
- Pepper, to taste
- Optional toppings: cherry tomatoes, radish slices, feta cheese, red pepper flakes

Tips for Success:

- **Choosing Avocados:** For immediate use, choose avocados that feel slightly soft when gently pressed. If you plan to use them later, select firmer ones and let them ripen at room temperature.
- **Customization:** Feel free to add other toppings like a poached egg for extra protein or some hot sauce for a kick.

It is recommended to use whole grain bread. The extra fiber found in whole wheat bread helps with digestion and contributes to a feeling of fullness. This can help reduce overall calorie intake.

METHOD

Step 1: Place the slices of bread in a toaster and toast them to your preferred crispiness. You can also toast the slices of bread on the preheated dry skillet.

Step 2: While the bread is toasting, cut the avocado in half, remove the pit, and scoop out the flesh into a bowl.

Step 3: Mash the Avocado: Use a fork to mash the avocado until it's creamy but still has some chunks. Drizzle with olive oil, and season with salt and pepper.

Step 5: Assemble the Toast: Spread the mashed avocado evenly over the toasted bread. Add any optional toppings you like.

Step 6: Enjoy your avocado toast immediately for the best flavor and texture.

Per Serving:

- **Calories:** 400 kcal
- **Protein:** 6 g
- **Fat:** 30 g (mostly healthy monounsaturated fat)

Carbohydrates: 29 g
Fiber: 13 g

NOTES

RATING

DIFFICULTY

Smoothie Bowl

PREP 10 MIN

COOK 0 MIN

1 SERVE

Benefits of Smoothie Bowl

Berries are known for their high antioxidant levels.

Will help fight inflammation and support immune health.

Greek yogurt adds a protein boost

For growth and muscle repair.

The natural sugars in **fruits**

provide quick energy.

The fiber from the fruits and optional chia seeds

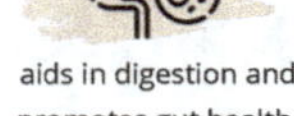

aids in digestion and promotes gut health.

Ingredients & Tools

- 1 cup frozen mixed berries (blueberries, strawberries, raspberries)
- 1 frozen banana, sliced
- 1/2 cup unsweetened almond milk (or any milk of choice)
- 1/2 cup Greek yogurt
- Toppings: sliced fresh fruits, granola, coconut flakes, chia seeds, honey (optional)

Tips for Success

Get Creative: Choose toppings based on what you like or need nutritionally. This can include a variety of nuts for healthy fats, seeds for fiber, or different fruits for vitamins.

It is recommended to start the day with eating the smoothie bowl for energy or refuel post-exercise thanks to its blend of carbohydrates and protein. However, consuming it late at night might not be ideal due to its typically high sugar content which can impact blood sugar levels before sleep.

METHOD

Step 1: In a blender, combine the frozen berries, banana, almond milk, and Greek yogurt. Blend until smooth.

Step 2: Pour the smoothie mixture into a bowl.

Arrange your chosen toppings over the smoothie base creatively.

Step 3: Drizzle with honey for added sweetness, if desired. Serve immediately and enjoy!

How to Blend:

1. **Freeze Your Fruits.** Using frozen fruits not only keeps the smoothie cold and thick without needing ice but also ensures a creamy texture. Make sure to cut fruits into smaller pieces before freezing for easier blending.
2. **Layer Smartly.** Start by adding liquids (such as water, milk, or juice) to your blender first. This helps create a vortex that pulls the solid ingredients down towards the blades, resulting in a smoother blend.
3. **Gradually Increase Speed**: Begin blending on a low speed to chop the ingredients, then gradually increase to high speed to achieve a smooth texture. This step-wise approach helps manage the strain on your blender's motor and can prevent jamming of the blades.
4. **Add More Liquids if Needed:** If the smoothie is too thick or the blender sounds strained, pause blending and add a little more liquid. Stir the mixture with a spoon or shake the blender container to redistribute the ingredients before continuing.

Per Serving:

- **Calories:** 250-280 calories
- **Total Carbohydrates:** 32-36 grams
- **Dietary Fiber:** 1-2 grams
- **Sugars:** 8-10 grams

Protein: 6-7 grams
Total Fat: 11-13 grams
Cholesterol: 50-55 mg
Sodium: 400-450 mg

NOTES

RATING

DIFFICULTY

Breakfast Tacos

PREP 5 MIN

COOK 10 MIN

2 SERVES

Benefits of Breakfast Tacos

Eggs are high in protein, vitamin B12, and choline.

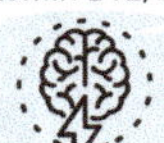

To stay smart.

Contain lutein and zeaxanthin, antioxidants

For Eye Health.

Avocado is a superfood. It contains vitamins C, E, K, and B-6, as well as riboflavin, niacin, folate, pantothenic acid, magnesium, and potassium.

To have healthy skin, hair, and nails.

Will help fight inflammation and support immune health.

To grow muscles.

Ingredients & Tools

- 4 small corn or flour tortillas
- 4 large eggs
- 1/2 cup shredded cheddar cheese
- 1/2 cup cooked and crumbled sausage or bacon (optional)
- 1 small avocado, diced
- 1/4 cup fresh salsa
- 1/4 cup sour cream (optional)
- Salt and pepper, to taste
- 1 tablespoon olive oil or butter
- Fresh cilantro, chopped (for garnish)
- Lime wedges (for serving)

It is recommended to opt for whole grain or corn tortillas over refined flour tortillas to increase your intake of fiber and nutrients. For healthier options, use lean proteins like chicken, turkey, lean beef, or fish as the base for your tacos.

Tips for Success

Ingredient Prep: Prepare all your toppings before you start cooking the eggs so everything is ready to assemble quickly.

Customization: Encourage creativity by setting up a taco bar where everyone can choose their own toppings, such as different types of cheese, vegetables, and sauces.

METHOD

Step 1: Cook the Eggs: In a skillet, heat the olive oil or melt the butter over medium heat. Beat the eggs in a bowl, season with salt and pepper, and pour into the skillet. Stir gently until the eggs are softly scrambled but still slightly runny.

Step 2: Cook the bacon or sausages according to package instruction in a skillet over medium heat until crispy. Remove from skillet and set aside.

Step 3: Warm the Tortillas: Heat the tortillas in a separate pan or directly over the stove flame until they are warm and slightly charred at the edges.

Step 4: Place the warm tortillas on plates. Divide the scrambled eggs among the tortillas. Top each with cheese, crumbled sausage or bacon (if using), and diced avocado.

Step 5: Spoon salsa and a dollop of sour cream on each taco. Garnish with chopped cilantro and serve with lime wedges on the sides.

Per Serving:

- **Calories:** Approximately 500-600 kcal (varies with toppings)
- **Protein:** 20-25 g
- **Fat:** 30-35 g
- **Carbohydrates:** 35-40 g
- **Fiber:** 5-7 g

NOTES

RATING

DIFFICULTY

Fluffy Sweet Pancakes

PREP 10 MIN | COOK 15 MIN | 2 SERVES (4 PANCAKES)

Benefits of Fluffy Pancakes

Using **whole wheat flour** instead of all-purpose flour

will be beneficial for digestive health.

6 grams of **protein** in each pancake

for growth and muscle repair.

Pancakes are primarily made from carbohydrates

to quickly energize you.

Milk in pancakes - source of calcium

for strong bones and teeth.

Ingredients & Tools

- 2 large eggs, separated into yolks and whites
- 1/4 cup sugar
- 1/2 cup milk
- 3/4 cup cake flour (or all-purpose flour sifted)
- 1/2 teaspoon baking powder
- 1/4 teaspoon cream of tartar (or a squeeze of lemon juice)
- Butter for cooking
- Maple syrup, honey, or fruit compote for serving
- Powdered sugar for dusting (optional)
- Pan
- Mixer or whisker

It is recommended to choose whole wheat flour instead of the white kinds to help your body run better and not gain extra weight. Limit your daily flour consumption to ensure you're not overloading on simple carbohydrates, which can contribute to weight gain and fluctuations in blood sugar levels.

Tips for Success

Gentle Folding: Use a spatula to fold the egg whites into the batter gently. This helps maintain the airiness that gives these pancakes their signature fluffiness.

Low and Slow Cooking: Cook the pancakes slowly on low heat to ensure they cook through without burning. The lid helps to steam the pancakes, contributing to their height and fluffiness.

METHOD

Step 1: Separate egg whites from yolks. Gently crack the shell over a bowl, carefully pull the shell apart into two halves. Allow the white to drain into the bowl by transferring the yolk back and forth between the two shell halves until all the white has fallen into the bowl.

Make sure that the bowls and any tools you use are clean and completely dry. Even a small amount of water or fat can prevent the egg whites from whipping properly.

Step 2: Prep the Egg Whites: In a clean, dry bowl, beat the egg whites with cream of tartar until foamy. Gradually add sugar while continuing to beat until stiff peaks form.

Step 3: Make the Batter: In another bowl, whisk together the egg yolks and milk. Sift in the flour and baking powder and mix until smooth.

Step 4: Fold in Egg Whites: Gently fold the whipped egg whites into the yolk mixture, taking care not to deflate the whites.

Step 5: Heat a non-stick skillet over low heat and brush with a little butter. Spoon the batter into the skillet to form 3-inch wide pancakes. Cover with a lid and cook for about 5 minutes, until the bottom is golden and the top surface is slightly set. Flip carefully and cook for another 3-5 minutes. Serve the pancakes warm with your choice of maple syrup, honey, or fruit compote and a dusting of powdered sugar if desired.

Per Serving:

- **Calories:** Approximately 300-350 kcal
- **Protein:** 8-10 g
- **Fat:** 5-7 g

Carbohydrates: 50-55 g
Fiber: 1-2 g

NOTES | **RATING** | **DIFFICULTY**

Hash Browns

PREP 5 MIN

COOK 15 MIN

2 SERVING

Benefits of hash browns

Butter/Oil provides fats

to quickly energize you.

Introducing **Greek Yogurt** will add protein value

for growth and muscle repair.

Potatoes: A good source of vitamins C and B6, potassium, and dietary fiber

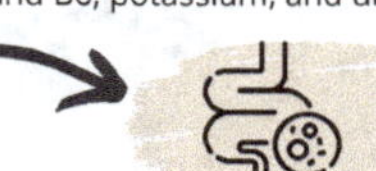

aids in digestion and promotes gut health.

promote heart health

Ingredients & Tools

- 2 large russet potatoes
- 2 tablespoons butter or oil
- Salt, to taste
- Pepper, to taste
- Optional: onion powder, garlic powder, or paprika for extra flavor
- Greek yogurt (or any other sauce)

Tips for Success:

- **Moderate Heat:** Keep the heat at a medium-high level to ensure that the potatoes get crispy without burning.
- **Be Patient:** Allow the hash browns to form a crust before flipping. Rushing this process can break them apart.

It is recommended using healthier cooking methods like baking or using minimal amounts of healthier oils (such as olive oil) to reduce the amount of saturated fat and calories. Be mindful of portion sizes since hash browns are high in calories

METHOD

Step 1: Prepare the potatoes: Peel the potatoes and grate them using the large holes of a box grater.

Step 2: Place the grated potatoes in a colander and rinse under cold water until the water runs clear. This removes excess starch. Squeeze out as much water as possible using your hands or a clean kitchen towel.

Step 3: Dry the potatoes well with paper towels. Removing as much moisture as possible from the potatoes is crucial for achieving crispy hash browns. Transfer the dried potatoes to a mixing bowl. Add salt, pepper, and any optional spices like onion powder or paprika, and mix well.

Step 5: Heat butter or oil in a large non-stick skillet over medium-high heat. Once hot, add the potato mixture, pressing it down firmly into the pan to form an even layer. Cook for about 5-7 minutes per side or until each side is crispy and golden brown.

Step 6: Remove the hash browns from the skillet, cut into wedges, and serve immediately with Greek yogurt or your favorite dipping sauce.

Per Serving:

- **Calories:** 250 kcal
- **Protein:** 3 g
- **Carbohydrates:** 34 g

Fat: 12 g
Carbohydrates: 34 g
Fiber: 3 g

NOTES

RATING

DIFFICULTY

Banana Oatmeal Muffins

PREP 5 MIN

COOK 20 MIN

12 SERVING

Benefits of Banana Oatmeal Muffins

Bananas: High in potassium and vitamins

promote heart health

These muffins are low in fat due to the use of **applesauce** instead of oil

to stay fit

The use of **whole wheat flour and oats** provides a good source of fiber

aid in digestion and promotes gut health.

Eggs are high in protein, vitamin B12, and choline

to stay smart.

Ingredients & Tools

- 1 1/2 cups whole wheat flour
- 1 cup rolled oats
- 1/3 cup brown sugar or honey
- 2 teaspoons baking powder
- 1 teaspoon baking soda
- 1/2 teaspoon salt
- 1 teaspoon cinnamon
- 3 ripe bananas, mashed
- 1/3 cup unsweetened applesauce
- 1/2 cup milk (dairy or non-dairy)
- 2 eggs
- 1 teaspoon vanilla extract
- Optional: nuts, chocolate chips, or dried fruit for mix-ins

Tips for Success:

Incorporate Nuts: Adding nuts provides healthy fats and protein, which can help increase satiety and provide energy.

Serve with Protein: Pair a muffin with Greek yogurt or a glass of milk to balance the meal and prolong fullness.

It is recommended to consume muffins in moderation, particularly if additional sweeteners or mix-ins are used. Limit your daily flour consumption to ensure you're not overloading on simple carbohydrates, which can contribute to weight gain and fluctuations in blood sugar levels.

METHOD

Step 1: Preheat Oven: Preheat your oven to 375°F (190°C) and line a muffin tin with paper liners or lightly grease it.

Step 2: Mix Dry Ingredients: In a large bowl, combine whole wheat flour, oats, brown sugar, baking powder, baking soda, salt, and cinnamon.

Step 3: Combine Wet Ingredients: In another bowl, whisk together the mashed bananas, applesauce, milk, eggs, and vanilla extract.

Step 4: Combine Mixtures: Add the wet ingredients to the dry ingredients, stirring just until combined. Fold in any optional mix-ins like nuts or chocolate chips.

Step 5: Bake: Spoon the batter into the prepared muffin tin, filling each cup about 3/4 full. Bake for 18-20 minutes, or until a toothpick inserted into the center of a muffin comes out clean.

Step 6: Let the muffins cool in the pan for 5 minutes, then transfer to a wire rack to cool completely.

Per Serving:

- **Calories:** 150 kcal
- **Protein:** 4 g
- **Fat:** 2 g

Carbohydrates: 30 g
Fiber: 3 g

NOTES

RATING

DIFFICULTY

Eggs Benedict Sandwich

PREP 10 MIN

COOK 10 MIN

2 SERVING

Benefits of Eggs Benedict Sandwich

Eggs and Canadian bacon provide a good source of protein

To stay strong and fit.

To grow muscles.

The use of **whole wheat flour and oats** provides a good source of fiber

aids in digestion and promotes gut health.

Eggs are high in protein, vitamin B12, and choline.

To stay smart.

Ingredients & Tools

- 2 English muffins, split and toasted
- 4 slices of Canadian bacon or ham
- 4 large eggs
- 1 tablespoon white vinegar (for poaching eggs)
- For the Hollandaise Sauce:
- 2 egg yolks
- 1 tablespoon lemon juice
- 1/2 cup unsalted butter, melted
- Pinch of salt

It is recommended to consume English muffins in moderation. Limit your daily flour consumption to ensure you're not overloading on simple carbohydrates, which can contribute to weight gain and fluctuations in blood sugar levels.

Tips for Success:

Fresh Eggs: Use the freshest eggs you can find, as they hold their shape better when poached.

Simmer, Don't Boil: Keep the water at a gentle simmer. Boiling water can break up the egg whites.

Vinegar: Add a splash of vinegar to the water. It helps the egg whites coagulate more quickly.

Whirlpool: Stir the water to create a gentle whirlpool before dropping the egg in. This helps the egg white wrap around the yolk.

METHOD

Step 1: Prepare Hollandaise Sauce: In a blender, combine egg yolks, lemon juice, salt, and cayenne pepper. Blend until light and frothy. Slowly add the melted butter while blending until the sauce thickens. Set aside and keep warm.

To make Hollandaise sauce without a blender, whisk egg yolks, lemon juice, salt, and cayenne in a heatproof bowl over simmering water, slowly add melted butter, and continue whisking until the sauce thickens.

Step 2: Poach the Eggs:
Bring a pot of water to a simmer and add vinegar. Crack each egg into a small cup, then gently pour it into the simmering water.
Cook for about 3-4 minutes until the whites are set but yolks remain runny. Remove with a slotted spoon.

Step 3: Assemble the Sandwich:
Toast the English muffins and warm the Canadian bacon (if using) in a skillet.
Place a slice of bacon on each muffin half, top with a poached egg, and drizzle with Hollandaise sauce.

Per Serving:

- **Calories:** 600 kcal
- **Protein:** 25 g
- **Fat:** 45 g
- **Carbohydrates:** 30 g
- **Fiber:** 2 g

NOTES

RATING

DIFFICULTY

Banana Bread

PREP 10 MIN | COOK 60 MIN | 1 LOAF (about 12 slices)

Benefits of Banana Bread

Bananas: High in potassium and vitamins

promote heart health.

Nuts (if added): Offer healthy fats, protein, and fiber

To stay energized.

The use of **whole wheat flour** provides a good source of fiber

aids in digestion and promotes gut health.

Eggs are high in protein, vitamin B12, and choline.

To stay smart.

Ingredients & Tools

- 2 cups all-purpose flour (or substitute half with whole wheat flour for added fiber)
- 1 teaspoon baking soda
- 1/4 teaspoon salt
- 1/2 teaspoon cinnamon
- 1/2 cup unsalted butter, melted and cooled
- 3/4 cup brown sugar
- 2 large eggs, beaten
- 2 1/3 cups mashed overripe bananas (about 4-5 medium bananas)
- 1 teaspoon vanilla extract
- Optional: 1/2 cup walnuts or pecans, chopped

It is recommended to consume banana bread in moderation, Limit your daily flour consumption to ensure you're not overloading on simple carbohydrates, which can contribute to weight gain and fluctuations in blood sugar levels.

Tips for Success:

Sugar Reduction: Consider reducing the sugar or using alternatives like honey or maple syrup, which may lower the glycemic index of the bread.

Whole Grains: Use whole wheat flour for half of the all-purpose flour to increase the fiber content, which aids in digestion and prolongs satiety.

Variety: Incorporate different fruits or nuts to vary the nutrient profile and flavors, such as adding blueberries for antioxidants or substituting applesauce for some of the butter for less saturated fat.

METHOD

Step 1: Preheat Oven and Prepare Pan: Preheat your oven to 350°F (175°C). Grease a 9x5 inch loaf pan or line it with parchment paper.

Step 2: Dry Ingredients: In a large bowl, whisk together the flour, baking soda, salt, and cinnamon.

Step 3: Wet Ingredients: In another bowl, mix the melted butter and brown sugar. Add the beaten eggs, mashed bananas, and vanilla extract; mix well.

Step 2: Combine Mixtures: Pour the banana mixture into the flour mixture; stir just to moisten. Fold in nuts if using.

Step 3: Pour batter into the prepared loaf pan. Bake in the preheated oven for about 60 minutes, or until a toothpick inserted into the center of the loaf comes out clean.

Step 4: Let bread cool in the pan for 10 minutes, then turn out onto a wire rack to cool completely. Serve warm.

Per Serving:

- **Calories:** 210 kcal
- **Protein:** 3 g
- **Fat:** 8 g

Carbohydrates: 34 g
Fiber: 1 g

NOTES

RATING

DIFFICULTY

Sausage Rolls

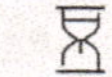

PREP 10 MIN | COOK 25 MIN | 5 SERVES

Benefits of Sausage Rolls

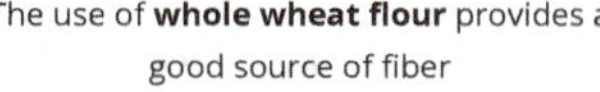
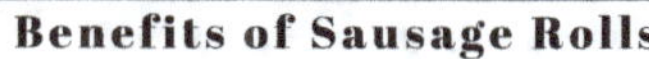

The use of **whole wheat flour** provides a good source of fiber

aids in digestion and promotes gut health.

Mustard: Adds flavor with minimal calories, and contains antioxidants

To stay fit.

Sausage provides a good source of protein

for muscle growth and repair

Onion and Garlic: Both contain antioxidants and compounds that help reduce inflammation

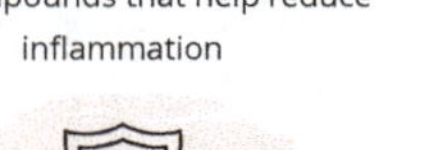

To support immune system

Ingredients & Tools

- 1 pound (450g) pork sausage meat (or substitute with turkey or chicken sausage for a leaner option)
- 1 sheet of puff pastry, thawed
- 1 small onion, finely chopped
- 2 cloves garlic, minced
- 1 tablespoon fresh herbs (such as parsley, thyme, or sage), chopped
- 1 teaspoon mustard (optional)
- Salt and pepper, to taste
- 1 egg, beaten (for egg wash)
- Optional: sesame seeds or poppy seeds for garnish

It is recommended when choosing the right sausages opting for sausages made from lean meats like turkey or chicken instead of pork or beef. Limit your daily flour consumption to ensure you're not overloading on simple carbohydrates, which can contribute to weight gain and fluctuations in blood sugar levels.

Tips for Success:

Keep the Pastry Cold: Puff pastry works best when it's cold. Handle it as little as possible with your hands to prevent it from warming up and becoming greasy. If the pastry becomes too soft while you are working with it, pop it back into the refrigerator for a few minutes to firm up.

Seal Properly: Ensure the edges of the pastry are well sealed to prevent the meat from leaking out during baking. Light brushing with an egg wash can help seal the pastry edges together.

Choose Sausages: The shorter the list of ingredients, the better. Look for sausages that contain mostly meat with few additives. Try to find sausages labeled as "low sodium" or check the nutritional information to choose options with less salt.

METHOD

Step 1: Preheat Oven and Prepare Baking Sheet: Preheat your oven to 400°F (200°C). Line a baking sheet with parchment paper.

Step 2: Prepare Sausages: In a bowl, combine sausages, chopped onion, minced garlic, herbs, mustard (if using), salt, and pepper. Mix until well combined.

Step 3: Prepare Puff Pastry:
Roll out the puff pastry on a lightly floured surface to a rectangle about 1/4 inch thick. Cut the pastry into two long strips.

Step 4: Assemble Sausage Rolls:
Divide the sausage mixture and shape into long logs down the center of each pastry strip.
Brush the edges of the pastry with beaten egg, then roll the pastry over the sausage, sealing the edge.

Step 5: Cut and Bake:
Cut each long roll into 6 pieces. Place on the prepared baking sheet, seam side down.
Brush the tops with more beaten egg and sprinkle with sesame or poppy seeds if desired.
Bake for 20-25 minutes, or until golden brown and cooked through.

Step 6: Serve: Allow to cool slightly before serving. Enjoy warm.

Per Serving:

- **Calories:** 250 kcal
- **Protein:** 10 g
- **Fat:** 18 g (varies with the type of sausage used)

Carbohydrates: 15 g
Fiber: 1 g

NOTES

RATING

DIFFICULTY

Cereal with Milk

PREP 5 MIN

COOK 0 MIN

1 SERVE

Benefits of Cereal with Milk

Milk: Offers a good source of protein, calcium, and vitamin D for strong bones and teeth.

Fruits and Nuts: Vitamins, antioxidants, and healthy fats help fight inflammation and support immune health.

Whole Grains: Provide essential nutrients such as fiber aids in digestion and promotes gut health.

For stable blood sugar.

Ingredients & Tools

- 1 cup of whole-grain cereal (choose a type with low sugar and high fiber)
- 1 cup of milk (dairy or a plant-based alternative like almond, soy, or oat milk)
- Optional toppings: Fresh fruits (such as berries or sliced bananas), nuts, or a sprinkle of cinnamon

Tips for Success:

Choose Low Sugar Cereal: Opt for cereals with less than 5 grams of sugar per serving to avoid unnecessary sugar intake.

High Fiber Content: Look for cereals that provide at least 3 grams of fiber per serving to promote satiety and digestive health.

Milk Alternatives: If using plant-based milk, choose fortified versions to ensure you're getting adequate calcium and vitamin D.

It is recommended to be mindful of portion sizes, as cereal calories can add up quickly, especially with added toppings. With the right ichoices of cereal and toppings, it can be a healthy and satisfying meal

METHOD

Step 1: Prepare the Cereal: Pour one cup of your chosen whole grain cereal into a bowl.

Step 2: Add Milk: Add one cup of milk to the bowl.

Step 4: Add Toppings: Top with fresh fruits, nuts, or cinnamon if desired.

Step 5: Serve: Enjoy immediately for the best texture and taste.

Per Serving:

- **Calories:** 200-300 kcal
- **Protein:** 8-10 g
- **Fat:** 2-8 g (varies with type of milk)

Carbohydrates: 30-40 g
Fiber: 4-6 g

NOTES

RATING

DIFFICULTY

Granola Bar

PREP 10 MIN

COOK 20 MIN

12 SERVES = 12 BARS

Benefits of Granola Bar

Dried Fruits: Contribute natural sweetness and fiber while being rich in antioxidants.

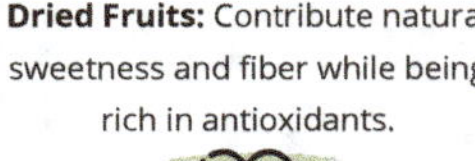

promote heart health.

Nuts and Seeds: Offer healthy fats, proteins, and various essential minerals

Help fight inflammation and support immune health.

Oats: Provide a good source of soluble fiber and carbs

To quickly energize you.

For stable blood sugar.

Ingredients & Tools

- 2 cups rolled oats
- 1/2 cup mixed nuts, chopped (such as almonds, walnuts, pecans)
- 1/4 cup seeds (such as pumpkin seeds or sunflower seeds)
- 1/4 cup honey or maple syrup
- 1/4 cup unsweetened applesauce
- 1/4 cup peanut butter or almond butter
- 1/2 cup dried fruit (such as cranberries, raisins, or chopped apricots)
- 1 teaspoon vanilla extract
- 1/2 teaspoon cinnamon
- 1/4 teaspoon salt

Tips for Success:

Proper Ingredient Ratios:

Ensure a good balance between dry and wet ingredients. Too much of the wet ingredients can make the bars too sticky or unable to hold together, while too little may result in crumbly bars.

It is recommended to be mindful of portion sizes. Even though granola bars are nutritious, they are also calorie-dense. Enjoy them in moderation, particularly if you are watching your caloric intake. Opt for natural sweeteners like honey or maple syrup and be cautious with the amount to keep sugar content lower.

METHOD

Step 1: Preheat your oven to 350°F (175°C). Line an 8-inch square baking pan with parchment paper, leaving some overhang for easy removal.

Step 2: Toast Oats and Nuts: Spread oats and nuts on a baking sheet and toast in the oven for about 10 minutes, stirring occasionally, until lightly golden.

Step 3: In a large bowl, combine the toasted oats and nuts with seeds and dried fruit. In a separate small saucepan over low heat, stir together honey, applesauce, nut butter, vanilla extract, cinnamon, and salt until smooth and well combined.

Step 4: Combine Wet and Dry Ingredients: Pour the wet mixture over the dry ingredients and stir until everything is well coated.

Step 5: Press into Pan: Transfer the mixture to the prepared pan and press down firmly with the back of a spoon or your hands to ensure the bars will hold together after baking.

Step 6: Bake for 20 minutes or until the edges are golden brown. Let cool completely in the pan before lifting out and cutting into bars.

Per Serving:

- **Calories:** 180 kcal
- **Protein:** 4 g
- **Fat:** 8 g
- **Carbohydrates:** 24 g
- **Fiber:** 3 g

NOTES

RATING

DIFFICULTY

Cinnabon rolls

PREP 2 HOURS | COOK 30 MIN | 8 SERVES

Benefits of Cinnabon rolls

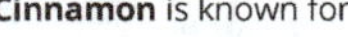

Cinnamon is known for

fighting inflammation

helping regulate blood sugar levels.

Cinnabon is high in calories, primarily from fats and carbohydrates

To quickly energize you

Milk provides calcium for bone health and protein

For strong bones and teeth

Ingredients & Tools

Dough:

- 1 cup warm milk (about 110°F or 45°C)
- 2 eggs, room temperature
- 1/3 cup unsalted butter, melted
- 4 1/2 cups all-purpose flour
- 1 teaspoon salt
- 1/2 cup granulated sugar
- 2 1/2 teaspoons instant yeast

Filling:

- 1 cup brown sugar, packed
- 3 tablespoons ground cinnamon
- 1/3 cup unsalted butter, softened

Cream Cheese Icing:

- 6 tablespoons unsalted butter, softened
- 1 1/2 cups powdered sugar
- 1/4 cup cream cheese, softened
- 1/2 teaspoon vanilla extract
- 1/8 teaspoon salt

Tips for Success

- Ensure the milk is warm but not hot to the touch to activate the yeast without killing it.
- If the dough is too sticky, add a little more flour while kneading.
- Roll the dough tightly when forming the log to prevent the filling from leaking out.

It is recommended to enjoy these treats occasionally due to high sugar and fat content. Be aware of portion sizes, especially when consuming rich desserts.

METHOD

Step 1: In the bowl of a stand mixer fitted with the dough hook attachment, dissolve the sugar in warm milk. Sprinkle yeast over the milk and let it sit for 5-10 minutes until frothy.

Add the eggs, butter, salt, and flour to the yeast mixture. Mix on low speed until well combined, then increase to medium and knead until the dough is smooth and elastic about 5-7 minutes, or knead by hand.

Place the dough in a lightly oiled bowl, cover with plastic wrap, and let rise in a warm place until doubled in size, about 1 to 1.5 hours.

Step 2: In a small bowl, combine brown sugar and cinnamon.

Step 3: Once the dough has risen, turn it out onto a lightly floured surface and roll it into a 16x21-inch rectangle. Spread the softened butter over the dough, leaving a 1-inch margin at the edges. Sprinkle the cinnamon-sugar mixture evenly over the butter. Starting with a long edge, roll the dough into a tight log and pinch the seam to seal. Cut the log into 12 equal slices using a sharp knife or dental floss. Arrange the slices cut side up in a greased 9x13 inch baking dish. Cover with a damp towel and let them rise for 30 minutes.

Step 4: Preheat your oven to 350°F (175°C).

Bake the rolls in the preheated oven until golden brown, about 18-20 minutes.

Step 5: While the rolls are baking, beat together cream cheese, butter, powdered sugar, vanilla extract, and salt in a bowl until fluffy.

Spread generously over the rolls while they are still warm so the icing melts into them.

Allow the rolls to cool slightly in the pan before serving warm

NOTES

RATING

DIFFICULTY

Per Serving:

- **Calories:** 460 kcal
- **Protein:** 6 g
- **Fat:** 20 g
- **Carbohydrates:** 65 g
- **Fiber:** 2 g

Fruit Salad

PREP 15 MIN

COOK 0 MIN

4 SERVES

Benefits of Fruit Salad

Vitamins and Minerals: A wide range of vitamins such as vitamin C, A, and potassium support immune function.

For eye health.

Fruit salad is a great way to boost hydration to feel refreshed.

Fruit skins provide dietary fiber aid in digestion and promotes gut health.

Ingredients & Tools

- 1 cup strawberries, hulled and halved
- 1 cup blueberries
- 1 cup grapes, halved
- 1 banana, sliced
- 1 apple, cored and chopped
- 1 orange, peeled and sectioned
- Juice of 1 lime
- Optional: 1 tablespoon honey or a sprinkle of chopped fresh mint for extra flavor

Tips for Success:

- Include a variety of fruits to get a broad spectrum of nutrients. Each type of fruit brings its own set of nutrients and benefits.
- Pair the fruit salad with a source of protein like Greek yogurt or nuts to make a more balanced meal that includes protein and healthy fats.

It is recommended If using honey, use sparingly to keep the natural flavors of the fruits prominent and avoid adding excessive sugar.

METHOD

Step 1: Prepare the Fruit: Wash all the fruit thoroughly. Prepare each fruit as indicated (hulling, halving, slicing, chopping) and combine them in a large mixing bowl.

Step 2: Add Flavor Enhancers: Squeeze the lime juice over the fruit. Add honey if desired for a touch of sweetness or mint for a fresh flavor.

Step 3: Mix Gently: Toss the fruit gently to mix the flavors without breaking the softer fruits.

Step 4: Chill (Optional): Refrigerate the salad for about 30 minutes before serving to enhance the flavors and provide a refreshing taste.

Step 5: Serve the fruit salad in bowls or as part of a brunch spread.

Per Serving:

- **Calories:** 120 kcal
- **Protein:** 1 g
- **Fat:** 0.5 g

Carbohydrates: 30 g
Fiber: 5 g

NOTES

RATING

DIFFICULTY

Breakfast Burritos

PREP 5 MIN | COOK 15 MIN | 4 SERVES

Ingredients & Tools

- 4 large flour tortillas (opt for whole grain or whole wheat tortillas to help with digestion and provide longer-lasting energy.
- 8 eggs
- 1/2 cup milk
- 1 cup shredded cheddar cheese
- 1/2 pound cooked bacon or sausage, crumbled
- 1 bell pepper, diced
- 1 small onion, diced
- 1/2 cup fresh spinach, chopped
- Salt and pepper to taste
- Optional: salsa, sour cream, or guacamole for serving

Tips for Success

- Customize the sandwich with additional toppings like spinach, bell peppers, or onions.
- Cook the eggs according to your preference, but avoid overcooking to retain their nutritional value.

It is recommended to use turkey bacon or chicken sausage instead of regular pork for a leaner protein source that reduces the overall fat content. Look for sausages that contain mostly meat with few additives. The shorter the list of ingredients, the better. Try to find sausages labeled as "low sodium" or check the nutritional information to choose options with less salt.

METHOD

Step 1: Cook the Filling:
In a large skillet, sauté the onion and bell pepper until softened, about 5 minutes. Add the spinach and cook until wilted.

Step 2: In a bowl, whisk together the eggs and milk. Pour into the skillet with the vegetables. Cook, stirring occasionally, until the eggs are scrambled and set. Stir in the cooked bacon or sausage and cheddar cheese until well combined. Season with salt and pepper.

Step 3: Assemble the Burritos:
Warm the tortillas on a skillet or in the microwave to make them pliable. Spoon the egg mixture down the center of each tortilla. Fold the bottom up over the filling, then fold in the sides and roll up tightly.

Step 4: Serve the burritos warm with optional sides of salsa, sour cream, or guacamole.

Per Serving:

- **Calories:** 500 kcal
- **Protein:** 28 g
- **Fat:** 30 g
- **Carbohydrates:** 32 g
- **Fiber:** 2 g

NOTES

RATING

DIFFICULTY

Classic Blueberry Muffins

PREP 5 MIN

COOK 25 MIN

12 SERVES

Benefits of Blueberry Muffins

Blueberries: High in antioxidants, particularly anthocyanins

To fight inflammation.

To promote heart health.

Substitute half of the all-purpose flour with **whole wheat flour**

aids in digestion and promotes gut health.

Milk: Offers a good source of protein, calcium, and vitamin D

for strong bones and teeth.

Ingredients & Tools

- 1 1/2 cups all-purpose flour
- 3/4 cup granulated sugar
- 1/2 teaspoon salt
- 2 teaspoons baking powder
- 1/3 cup vegetable oil
- 1 large egg
- 1/3 cup milk
- 1 cup fresh blueberries
- Optional: 1 teaspoon vanilla extract for added flavor
- Muffin tin with paper liners or the cups

Tips for Success

- Introduce nuts like walnuts or almonds for added protein and healthy fats.
- Pair a muffin with a protein-rich food such as Greek yogurt or a glass of milk to balance the meal.

It is recommended to reduce the sugar by up to 1/4 cup or substituting some with honey or maple syrup for a healthier variant. Limit your daily flour consumption to ensure you're not overloading on simple carbohydrates, which can contribute to weight gain and fluctuations in blood sugar levels.

METHOD

Step 1: Preheat your oven to 400°F (200°C). Line a muffin tin with paper liners or grease the cups lightly.

Step 2: In a large bowl, whisk together flour, sugar, salt, and baking powder.

Step 3: In another bowl, mix the vegetable oil, egg, and milk together. Add vanilla extract if using.

Step 4: Pour the wet mixture into the dry ingredients and stir until just combined. Be careful not to overmix. into the dry ingredients and stir until just combined.

Step 5: Gently fold the blueberries into the batter.

Step 5: Spoon the batter into the prepared muffin tin, filling each cup about 3/4 full. Bake for about 20-25 minutes, or until a toothpick inserted into the center of a muffin comes out clean.

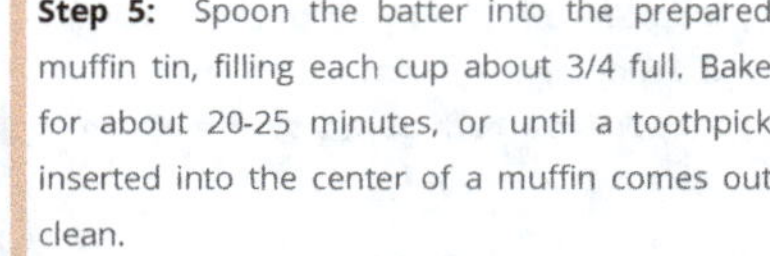

Step 6: Allow the muffins to cool in the pan for 5 minutes before transferring them to a wire rack to cool completely.

Per Serving:

- **Calories:** 180 kcal
- **Protein:** 2 g
- **Fat:** 7 g
- **Carbohydrates:** 28 g
- **Fiber:** 1 g

NOTES

RATING

DIFFICULTY

Croissants with Banana and Chocolate

PREP 30 MIN

COOK 15-20 MIN
(for baking)

8 SERVES

Benefits of Croissants with Banana and Chocolate

Bananas: Provide potassium and dietary fiber

aid in digestion and promotes gut health.

Puff pastry is high in calories, primarily from fats and carbohydrates

To quickly energize you.

Chocolate: Contains antioxidants

promote heart health.

Dark chocolate typically contains a higher percentage of cocoa compared to milk chocolate

to fight inflammation.

Ingredients & Tools

- 8 cut-in-half premade croissants or 1 sheet puff pastry, thawed and 1 egg, beaten (for egg wash)
- 2 ripe bananas, mashed
- 1/2 cup chocolate chips or chopped chocolate
- Optional: Powdered sugar for dusting

Tips for Success

- Complement a croissant with a side of fresh fruit or a protein-rich yogurt to balance the meal.
- Look for dark chocolate that contains at least 70% cocoa solids. Higher cocoa content generally means more antioxidants and less sugar.

It is recommended to enjoy these treats occasionally due to high sugar and fat content. Be aware of portion sizes, especially when consuming rich desserts. Opt for dark chocolate due to its higher content of cocoa solids and lower sugar levels.

METHOD

Step 1: If cooking from scratch Preheat your oven to 350°F (175°C).

Step 2: Prepare Puff Pastry: Roll out the puff pastry on a lightly floured surface into a 12x12 inch square. Cut into 8 triangles.

Step 3: Prepare Filling: In a bowl, mix together the mashed bananas and chocolate chips.

Step 4: Add Filling: Spoon a generous amount of the banana-chocolate mixture on the wider end of each triangle or cut-in-half premade croissants.

Step 5: Roll up each triangle from the wider end to the pointed tip, forming a croissant shape. Curve the ends slightly to form a crescent.

Step 6: Brush each croissant with a beaten egg.

Step 7: Bake: Place the croissants on the prepared baking sheet and bake for 15-20 minutes or until golden brown.

Step 8: Dust with powdered sugar and sprinkle some melted chocolate before serving, if desired.

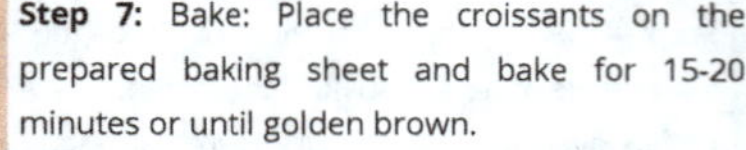

Per Serving:

- **Calories:** 300 kcal
- **Protein:** 5 g
- **Fat:** 18 g
- **Carbohydrates:** 34 g
- **Fiber:** 2 g

NOTES

RATING

DIFFICULTY

Bacon, Egg, and Cheese Biscuit

PREP 0 MIN

COOK 30 MIN

4 SERVES

Benefits of Bacon, Egg, and Cheese Biscuit

Cheese is a good source of calcium.

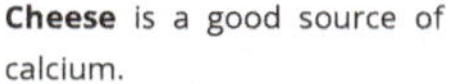

For strong bones and teeth.

Biscuit is high in calories, primarily from fats and carbohydrates.

To quickly energize you.

Eggs and bacon provide high-quality protein.

To stay fit.

For growth.

Ingredients & Tools

- 4 large eggs
- 4 slices of bacon
- 4 slices of cheddar cheese
- 4 homemade or store-bought buttermilk biscuits
- Salt and pepper to taste
- Optional: butter for biscuits, hot sauce or ketchup for serving

For homemade biscuits:

- 2 cups all-purpose flour
- 1 tablespoon baking powder
- 1 teaspoon salt
- 6 tablespoons cold unsalted butter, cubed
- 3/4 cup cold milk

Tips for Success

Scramble the eggs on low heat to keep them soft and moist. Overcooked eggs can become rubbery and less enjoyable. Ensure that the bacon is well-drained on paper towels to remove excess grease, which can make the biscuits soggy.

It is recommended to opt for whole grain biscuits to increase fiber content and nutritional value. Consider using turkey bacon for a lower fat option. Alternatively, you can pair this biscuit with a side of fresh fruit or vegetables for a more balanced meal.

METHOD

Step 1: Prepare the Biscuits:

If using store-bought, follow package instructions to bake or warm them.

If homemade, prepare your biscuits ahead of time:

1. Preheat your oven to 425°F (218°C).
2. In a large bowl, sift together the flour, baking powder, and salt.
3. Using a pastry cutter or your fingers, cut the butter into the flour until the mixture resembles coarse crumbs.
4. Make a well in the center of the flour mixture and pour in the cold milk. Stir just until the dough comes together. It should be sticky.

Step 2: Roll and Cut Dough:

Turn the dough out onto a floured surface and knead gently a few times. Handle the dough as little as possible to keep it light and flaky. Roll the dough to about 1-inch thickness. Use a biscuit cutter or a round glass to cut out biscuits.

2. Place biscuits on a parchment-lined baking sheet, making sure they just barely touch. Bake for 12-15 minutes or until they are golden brown on top.

Step 3: Cook the Bacon:

In a skillet over medium heat, cook the bacon until crispy. Remove from skillet and place on paper towels to drain the excess fat.

Step 4: Scramble the Eggs:

In the same skillet, reduce the heat to low. Beat the eggs with a pinch of salt and pepper. Pour into the skillet, cooking slowly and stirring frequently, until the eggs are softly scrambled.

Step 5: Assemble the Biscuits:

Slice each biscuit in half. Optionally butter each half. Place a slice of cheese on the bottom half, top with a portion of scrambled eggs, then add a slice of bacon, broken to fit. Cover with the top half of the biscuit. Serve immediately while warm, with hot sauce or ketchup if desired.

Per Serving:

- **Calories:** 450 kcal
- **Protein:** 22 g
- **Fat:** 26 g
- **Carbohydrates:** 34 g
- **Fiber:** 1 g

NOTES

RATING

DIFFICULTY

Vegetable Casserole

PREP 10 MIN

COOK 40 MIN

4-6 SERVES

Benefits of Vegetable Casserole

Broccoli and cauliflower are high in vitamins C and K, and fiber

aid in digestion and promotes gut health.

Support immune system

Cheese and milk provide calcium for bone health and protein.

For strong bones and teeth.

For muscle growth and repair.

Ingredients & Tools

- 1 cup broccoli florets
- 1 cup cauliflower florets
- 1 large carrot, sliced
- 1/2 cup milk
- 1 can (10.5 oz) cream of mushroom soup
- 1 cup shredded cheddar cheese
- Salt and pepper to taste
- Optional: 1/2 cup breadcrumbs for topping

Tips for Success

- **Even Cooking:** Cut vegetables into uniform sizes to ensure they cook evenly.
- **Season Well:** Don't forget to season the mixture well with salt and pepper before baking to enhance the natural flavors of the vegetables.
- **Test Doneness:** Check that the vegetables are tender by piercing them with a fork before removing from the oven.

It is recommended to use low-fat milk and reduced-fat cheese to decrease the overall fat content. Instead of mushroom soup, use fresh button mushrooms instead with broth, for a vegetarian green bean casserole, use vegetable broth.

METHOD

Step 1: Preheat your oven to 350°F (175°C).

Step 2: Wash the broccoli, cauliflower, and carrot. Cut them into bite-sized pieces.

Step 3: In a large mixing bowl, combine the cut vegetables, mushroom soup and milk. Stir until the vegetables are evenly coated. Season with salt and pepper to taste.

Step 4: Assemble the Casserole:
Transfer the vegetable and soup mixture into a greased 9x9 inch baking dish. Sprinkle the shredded cheese evenly over the top.
If using, sprinkle breadcrumbs on top of the cheese for a crispy finish.

Step 5: Bake in the preheated oven for 35-40 minutes, or until the vegetables are tender and the top is golden and bubbly. Allow the casserole to cool for a few minutes before serving.

Per Serving:

- **Calories:** 200 kcal
- **Protein:** 9 g
- **Fat:** 12 g
- **Carbohydrates:** 15 g
- **Fiber:** 3 g

NOTES

RATING

DIFFICULTY

Crepes

PREP 30 MIN

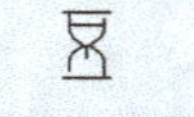
COOK 20 MIN

12 SERVES

Benefits of Crepes

Ingredients & Tools

- 1 cup all-purpose flour
- 2 cups milk
- 2 large eggs
- 1 tablespoon sugar (optional, for sweet crepes)
- 1/4 teaspoon salt
- 2 tablespoons melted butter, plus more for cooking
- Optional: 1/2 teaspoon vanilla extract (for sweet crepes) or herbs (for savory crepes)

Tips for Success

- **Consistent Heat:** Maintain a consistent medium heat to avoid burning the crepes.
- **Smooth Batter:** Ensure the batter is smooth and free of lumps for the best texture. A blender can be used to mix the batter quickly and efficiently.
- **Thin Pour:** Pour just enough batter to cover the bottom of the pan; the crepe should be very thin.

It is recommended to choose whole wheat flour instead of the white kinds to help your body run better and not gain extra weight. Limit your daily flour consumption to ensure you're not overloading on simple carbohydrates, which can contribute to weight gain and fluctuations in blood sugar levels.

METHOD

Step 1:
In a large mixing bowl, combine the flour, sugar (if making sweet crepes), and salt. In another bowl, whisk together the milk, eggs, and melted butter. Add vanilla extract if desired. Gradually add the wet ingredients to the dry ingredients, whisking continuously until the batter is smooth and free of lumps. The batter should be very liquid; if it seems too thick, add a little more milk.

Step 2: Rest the Batter:
Cover the batter and let it rest in the refrigerator for at least 30 minutes. This helps the flour absorb the liquid and can make the crepes more tender.

Step 3: Cook the Crepes:
Heat a non-stick skillet or crepe pan over medium heat. Lightly butter the pan.
Pour about 1/4 cup of batter into the center of the pan. Immediately tilt and swirl the pan to spread the batter evenly over the bottom.
Cook for about 1-2 minutes until the edges look dry and can be lifted with a spatula. Flip the crepe and cook for another 30 seconds to 1 minute on the other side.
Remove the crepe from the pan and keep it warm. Repeat with the remaining batter, adding more butter to the pan as needed.

Step 4: Serve:
Serve the crepes warm. They can be filled with a variety of fillings, such as:
Sweet Options: Jam, Nutella, honey, fresh fruit, whipped cream, or yogurt.
Savory Options: Ham, cheese, cooked eggs, sautéed vegetables, or meats.

Per Serving:

- **Calories:** 90 kcal
- **Protein:** 3 g
- **Fat:** 4 g
- **Carbohydrates:** 10 g

NOTES

RATING

DIFFICULTY

Breakfast Salad

PREP 20 MIN

COOK 0 MIN

4 SERVES

Benefits of Breakfast Salad

Eggs are rich in vitamins B12, D and A fnd choline

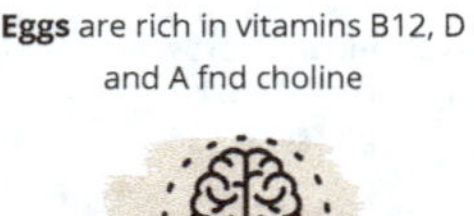

To stay smart.

Eggs contain lutein and zeaxanthin, antioxidants

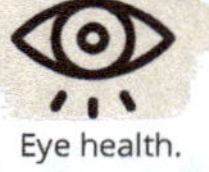

Eye health.

Avocado is a superfood. It contains vitamins C, E, K, and B-6, as well as riboflavin, niacin, folate, pantothenic acid, magnesium, and potassium.

To have healthy skin, hair, and nails.

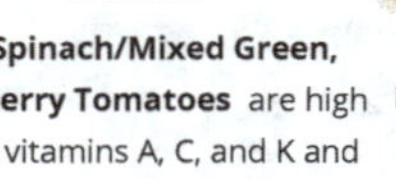

Spinach/Mixed Green, Cherry Tomatoes are high in vitamins A, C, and K and other antioxidants

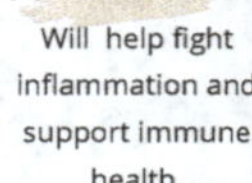

Will help fight inflammation and support immune health.

Ingredients & Tools

Salad:

- 4 cups fresh spinach or mixed greens
- 4 eggs (hard-boiled and sliced or poached)
- 1 avocado, sliced
- 1 cup cherry tomatoes, halved
- 1/2 cup cooked quinoa
- 1/4 cup crumbled feta cheese
- 1/4 cup almonds or walnuts, toasted
- Optional: 4 slices of cooked bacon, crumbled

Dressing:

- 2 tablespoons olive oil
- 1 tablespoon lemon juice
- 1 teaspoon Dijon mustard
- Salt and pepper to taste
- Optional: 1 teaspoon honey or maple syrup for sweetness

Tips for Success

- **Protein Variations:** You can swap out the bacon for smoked salmon or grilled chicken or keep it vegetarian.
- **Egg Cooking:** For a softer yolk, poach the eggs to your liking or opt for a soft-boiled egg instead of hard-boiled.

It is recommended to use fresh, high-quality ingredients for the best flavor and nutritional value. Adjust the dressing ingredients according to your taste preferences. More mustard for a sharper flavor, or more honey for sweetness.

METHOD

Step 1: Prepare the Eggs:
If hard-boiling, place eggs in a pot of water, bring to a boil, then cover and turn off the heat. Let sit for 10-12 minutes, then cool in ice water and peel. Slice the eggs.
For poached eggs, bring a pot of water to a gentle simmer, add a little vinegar, and crack each egg into the pot. Cook for 3-4 minutes, then remove with a slotted spoon.

Step 2: Prepare the Salad Base:
In a large bowl, combine the spinach or mixed greens, cherry tomatoes, and cooked quinoa. Arrange the sliced or poached eggs, sliced avocado, and crumbled bacon (if using) on top of the greens. Sprinkle with toasted almonds or walnuts and feta cheese.

Step 3: Mix the Dressing:
In a small bowl or jar, whisk together the olive oil, lemon juice, Dijon mustard, salt, and pepper. Add honey or maple syrup if you prefer a touch of sweetness.

Step 4: Dress the Salad:
Drizzle the dressing over the salad just before serving. Toss gently to combine or leave as is for guests to mix individually.
Serve the breakfast salad immediately, ensuring ingredients are fresh and vibrant.

Per Serving:

- **Calories:** 350 kcal
- **Protein:** 15 g
- **Fat:** 25 g
- **Carbohydrates:** 18 g
- **Fiber:** 6 g

NOTES

RATING

DIFFICULTY

Fries

PREP 10 MIN

COOK 30 MIN

4 SERVES

Benefits of Breakfast Salad

Potatoes: Provide a good source of vitamin C, vitamin B6, and potassium. They are naturally fat-free and offer fiber, especially with the skin on.

Aids in digestion and promotes gut health.

Olive Oil/Avocado Oil: Both oils are high in monounsaturated fats, which are heart-healthy fats that can help reduce bad cholesterol levels and lower the risk of heart disease and stroke.

Promote heart health.

Ingredients & Tools

- 4 large potatoes (Russet or Yukon Gold are preferred)
- 2 tablespoons olive oil (or use avocado oil for a higher smoke point)
- Salt to taste
- Optional seasonings: garlic powder, paprika, black pepper, or any herbs like rosemary or thyme

Tips for Success

- Even Slicing: Ensure all fries are cut to approximately the same thickness for uniform cooking.
- Spacing: Avoid overcrowding the baking sheet. Air should circulate around each fry, helping them become crispy.
- High Heat: High temperature is key to getting a crispy exterior without overcooking the inside.

It is recommended to consume fires in moderation due to their higher carbohydrate content. Pair fries with a protein source and vegetables for a balanced meal, such as a grilled chicken breast and a side salad.

METHOD

Step 1: Preheat your oven to 425°F (218°C). Line a baking sheet with parchment paper or a silicone baking mat for easy cleanup. Wash the potatoes thoroughly and pat them dry. You can peel them if you prefer, but leaving the skin on provides additional nutrients and texture.

Step 2: Cut the potatoes into strips about 1/4 inch thick for even cooking.

Toss the potato strips in a bowl with olive oil, and your chosen seasonings until evenly coated.

Step 3: Arrange on Baking Sheet:

Spread the fries in a single layer on the prepared baking sheet. Make sure they aren't overlapping to ensure they cook evenly.

Step 4: Bake in the preheated oven for 15 minutes, then flip the fries and continue baking for another 15 minutes or until they are golden and crisp. Sprinkle with a little more salt or additional seasonings if desired right after baking. Serve hot with ketchup, mayo, or a homemade aioli.

Per Serving:

- Calories: 250-300
- Protein: 4-5g
- Fat: 7-10g
- Carbohydrates: 45-50g
- Fiber: 3-4g
- Sodium: 300-400mg (varies based on the amount of salt used)

NOTES

RATING

DIFFICULTY

LUNCH
Grilled Cheese Sandwich

PREP 0 MIN

COOK 10 MIN

2 SERVES

Benefits of Grilled Cheese Sandwich

Ingredients & Tools

- 4 slices of bread (sourdough, whole grain, or white)
- 4 slices of cheese (cheddar, American, or your choice of meltable cheese)
- 2 tablespoons butter, room temperature
- Optional: additions like sliced tomatoes, cooked bacon, or basil leaves

Tips for Success

- **Butter is Key:** Room temperature butter spreads more easily and helps achieve a golden, crispy texture without burning.
- **Cheese Choices:** Use a good melting cheese for that classic stretchy texture. Combining cheeses can also add depth of flavor.
- **Additions:** Experiment with fillings like ham, tomato, or thin apple slices to enhance your sandwich without overwhelming the classic flavor.

It is recommended to limit your daily bread consumption to ensure you're not overloading on simple carbohydrates, which can contribute to weight gain and fluctuations in blood sugar level.

METHOD

Step 1:
Butter one side of each bread slice. Place the cheese (and any optional ingredients) between the non-buttered sides of two slices of bread to form sandwiches. Optionally, cut the sandwiches in half.

Step 2:
Heat a skillet or frying pan over medium heat. Medium heat allows the bread to get crispy without burning it while ensuring the cheese melts perfectly.

Step 3:
Place the sandwiches in the pan, buttered side down. Cook for about 3-4 minutes or until the bottom is golden brown and crispy. Lightly pressing the sandwich while grilling helps improve contact with the heat for an even crispy texture.

Step 4:
Flip carefully with a spatula and press down slightly to ensure even grilling. Cook for another 3-4 minutes or until the second side is golden brown and the cheese is melted.
Remove from the pan and let sit for a minute before cutting. Serve warm.

Per Serving:

- **Calories:** 400 kcal
- **Protein:** 15 g
- **Fat:** 22 g
- **Carbohydrates:** 34 g
- **Fiber:** 2 g

NOTES

RATING

DIFFICULTY

Chicken Nuggets

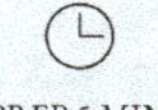
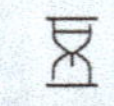

PREP 5 MIN | COOK 25 MIN | 4 SERVES

Benefits of Chicken Nuggets

Chicken provides choline, B vitamins and selenium

To stay smart.

For strong bones and teeth.

Chicken is a good source of high-quality protein

Muscle growth and repair.

Promote heart health.

Ingredients & Tools

- 1 pound (450g) boneless, skinless chicken breasts
- 1 cup all-purpose flour
- 1 teaspoon paprika
- 1 teaspoon garlic powder
- 1/2 teaspoon salt
- 1/4 teaspoon black pepper
- 2 large eggs, beaten
- 1 cup breadcrumbs
- Optional: 1/2 teaspoon onion powder or any other preferred seasoning
- Cooking oil for frying

It is recommended to enjoy nuggets in moderation as part of a balanced diet. Chicken nuggets are often fried and can be high in calories, fats, especially saturated fats, and sodium.

Tips for Success

- **Uniform Pieces:** Cut the chicken into even pieces to ensure that they cook uniformly.
- **Proper Oil Temperature:** For frying, make sure the oil is hot enough before adding the chicken. A thermometer can help; aim for about 350°F (177°C) to prevent the chicken from absorbing too much oil.
- **Drain Excess Oil:** If frying, drain the cooked nuggets on paper towels to remove excess oil.
- **Ensure Crispy Coating:** If baking, flipping the nuggets halfway through cooking helps achieve a more crispness.

METHOD

Step 1: Cut the chicken breasts into 1-2 inch pieces, ensuring they are roughly the same size for even cooking.

Step 2: In a shallow dish, combine the flour, paprika, garlic powder, salt, pepper, and optional onion powder. Place the beaten eggs in another shallow dish. Put the breadcrumbs in a third shallow dish.

Step 3: Dip each piece of chicken first into the flour mixture, shaking off excess.

Dip next into the beaten eggs.

Finally, coat well with breadcrumbs. Press the crumbs onto the chicken pieces to ensure they adhere well.

Step 4: Cook the Nuggets (Baking can significantly reduce the amount of fat and make them healthier without sacrificing taste).

For Frying: Heat oil in a large frying pan over medium heat. Fry the nuggets in batches, without overcrowding the pan, for about 3-4 minutes per side or until golden brown and the internal temperature reaches 165°F (74°C).

For Baking: Preheat oven to 400°F (200°C). Place nuggets on a greased baking sheet and spray or brush lightly with oil. Bake for 20-25 minutes, turning halfway through, until golden brown and cooked through.

Serve hot with your choice of dipping sauces, such as ketchup, barbecue sauce, honey mustard, or ranch dressing.

Per Serving (Frying) :

- **Calories:** 300 - 400 kcal
- **Protein:** 20-25g
- **Fat:** 20-25g

Carbohydrates: 20-25g
Fiber: 1-2 g

Per Serving (Baking) :

- **Calories:** 200 - 250 kcal
- **Protein:** 20-25g
- **Fat:** 5-10 g

Carbohydrates: 20-25g
Fiber: 1-2 g

NOTES

RATING

DIFFICULTY

Cheeseburger

 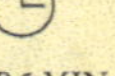
PREP 5 MIN

COOK 10 MIN

4 SERVES

Benefits of Cheeseburger

Cheese: Provides calcium and protein.

For strong bones and teeth.

Lettuce, tomatoes and onions contain necessary vitamins

to stay healthy.

Beef is a good source of high-quality protein and iron

muscle growth and repair.

To feel energized.

Ingredients & Tools

- 1 pound ground beef
- 4 slices of cheese (cheddar, American, or Swiss)
- 4 hamburger buns
- Salt and pepper to taste
- 4 lettuce leaves
- 1 tomato, sliced
- 4 tablespoons mayonnaise
- 4 teaspoons ketchup
- Optional: slices of onion, pickles

It is recommended to limit your daily bread consumption to ensure you're not overloading on simple carbohydrates, which can contribute to weight gain and fluctuations in blood sugar level. Opt for lean or extra-lean ground beef whenever possible. Look for ground beef that is labeled 90% lean or higher.

Tips for Success

- **Patty Thickness:** Don't press down on the patties while cooking, as this can cause them to dry out. Make a small indentation in the center to prevent them from puffing up.
- **Cheese Choice:** Use a good melting cheese like cheddar or American for that classic cheeseburger look and flavor.
- **Cooking Temperature:** Ensure the grill or skillet is hot before adding the patties to get a good sear on the outside while keeping the inside juicy.
- **Freshness:** Use fresh lettuce and tomatoes for the best texture and taste.

METHOD

Step 1: Prepare the Patties: Divide the ground beef into 4 equal portions. Form each portion into a round, flat patty that is about 1/2 inch thick. Season both sides of each patty with salt and pepper.

Step 2: Cook the Patties: Preheat a grill or skillet over medium-high heat. Lightly toast the hamburger buns on the grill or in a toaster. Then cook the patties for about 3-4 minutes on one side. Flip the patties, and immediately place a slice of cheese on each. Cook for another 3-4 minutes for medium doneness.

Step 3: Spread mayonnaise on the bottom buns. Place a lettuce leaf on each bun, followed by a slice of tomato and optionally onion and pickles.

Place the cooked patties with melted cheese on top of the vegetables. Add a teaspoon of ketchup on the patty.

Step 4: Cover with the top halves of the buns. Serve the cheeseburgers immediately while they are hot and the cheese is melted.

Per Serving:

- **Calories:** 600 kcal
- **Protein:** 30 g
- **Fat:** 40 g

Carbohydrates: 30 g
Fiber: 2 g

NOTES

RATING

DIFFICULTY

Tacos

PREP 20 MIN

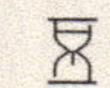
COOK 0 MIN

4 SERVES

Benefits of Tacos

Made from **whole grain corn**, corn tortillas are a good source of whole grains

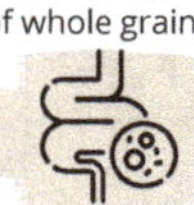

aid in digestion and promotes gut health.

Lettuce, tomatoes, and onions add fiber, vitamins, and minerals

to stay healthy.

Beef is a good source of high-quality protein and iron

for muscle growth and repair.

To feel energized.

Ingredients & Tools

- 1 pound ground beef (or substitute with ground chicken, turkey, or a plant-based alternative)
- 8 small corn or flour tortillas
- 1 tablespoon taco seasoning (homemade or store-bought)
- 1/2 cup water
- 1 cup shredded lettuce
- 1 cup diced tomatoes
- 1/2 cup shredded cheddar cheese
- 1/4 cup finely chopped onion
- 1/4 cup chopped cilantro
- Sour cream (for serving)
- Salsa (for serving)
- Lime wedges (for serving)
- Salt and pepper to taste

Tips for Success

Seasoning the Meat: Adjust the taco seasoning to your taste. If you like it spicier, add more chili powder or some cayenne pepper.

Keeping Tortillas Warm: Keeping tortillas warm wrapped in a cloth helps them stay pliable and warm until ready to serve.

Variety of Toppings: Feel free to add other toppings such as avocado, guacamole, or pickled jalapenos for more flavors and textures.

It is recommended to choose corn tortillas over regular ones because they are very low in fat, with less than 1 gram of fat per medium-sized tortilla. This makes them a lighter option compared to other types of bread and tortillas, such as flour tortillas, which are higher in fat.

METHOD

Step 1: Chop the onion and mix with ground beef. In a skillet over medium heat, cook the ground beef until it's no longer pink. Break the meat into small pieces with a spoon.

Drain any excess grease, then add the taco seasoning and water. Stir well and simmer until the water is absorbed and the meat is nicely flavored. Season with salt and pepper to taste.

Step 2: While the meat is cooking, prepare the toppings: shred the lettuce, dice the tomatoes, shred the cheese, and chop the cilantro.

Step 3: Warm the tortillas in a dry skillet over medium heat for about 30 seconds on each side, or until they are soft and pliable. Keep them warm by wrapping them in a clean cloth.

Step 4: Assemble the Tacos:

Spoon the cooked meat into the center of each tortilla. Top with lettuce, tomatoes, cheese, onion, and cilantro.

Add a dollop of sour cream and some salsa on top. Serve with a lime wedge for squeezing.

Per Serving:

- **Calories:** 450 kcal
- **Protein:** 26 g
- **Fat:** 22 g
- **Carbohydrates:** 34 g
- **Fiber:** 5 g

NOTES

RATING

DIFFICULTY

Turkey Sandwich

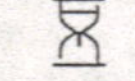

PREP 10 MIN | COOK 0 MIN | 2 SERVES

Benefits of Turkey Sandwich

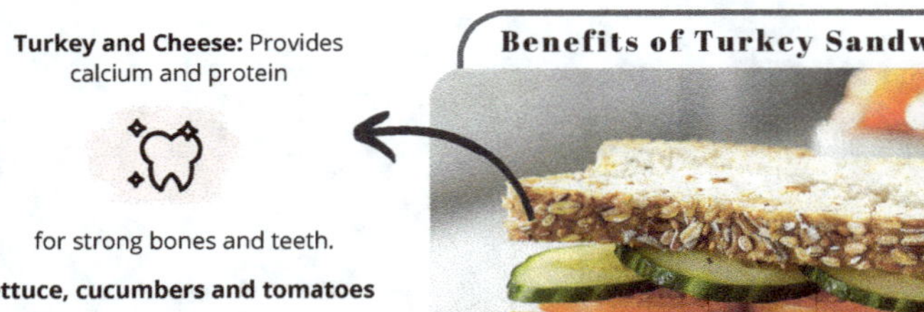

Turkey and Cheese: Provides calcium and protein for strong bones and teeth.

Lettuce, cucumbers and tomatoes contain necessary vitamins

to stay healthy.

Avocado is a superfood. It contains vitamins C, E, K, and B-6, as well as riboflavin, niacin, folate, pantothenic acid, magnesium, and potassium.

To have healthy skin, hair, and nails.

Whole Grain Bread: Offers fiber and nutrients if chosen over white bread

aids in digestion and promotes gut health

Ingredients & Tools

- 4 slices of whole grain bread
- 4 ounces (about 8 slices) of deli turkey breast
- 2 slices of cheddar or Swiss cheese
- 1 avocado, sliced
- 1 small tomato, sliced
- 1/2 cucumber, thinly sliced
- 4 lettuce leaves
- 2 tablespoons mayonnaise
- 1 tablespoon mustard
- Salt and pepper to taste

Tips for Success

Bread Selection: Opt for whole grain or whole wheat bread for added nutrients and fiber.

Variety of Toppings: Feel free to add or substitute toppings based on personal preferences. For example, bell peppers, onions, or sprouts can enhance the sandwich's flavor and nutritional profile.

It is recommended to limit your daily bread consumption to ensure you're not overloading on simple carbohydrates, which can contribute to weight gain. Look for turkey breast options with minimal ingredients. Ideally, the ingredient list should be short, primarily featuring turkey breast and perhaps water, salt, and natural seasonings. Avoid products with a long list of preservatives and additives like sodium nitrite or phosphates.

METHOD

Step 1: Prepare the Ingredients:

Wash the lettuce, tomato, and cucumber. Slice the tomato and cucumber thinly. Peel and slice the avocado.

Step 2: Assemble the Sandwich:

Spread mayonnaise on two slices of bread and mustard on the other two slices. On the mayonnaise-spread slices, layer the lettuce leaves, tomato slices, cucumber slices, turkey slices, and a slice of cheese.

Add a few slices of avocado on top, and season with a pinch of salt and pepper. Cover with the mustard-spread slices of bread.

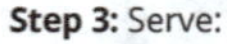

Step 3: Serve:

Cut the sandwiches in half if desired and serve immediately. Pair the sandwich with a side of fruit or yogurt to make it a balanced meal suitable for a teen's dietary needs.

Per Serving:

- **Calories:** 450 kcal
- **Protein:** 25 g
- **Fat:** 20 g

Carbohydrates: 40 g
Fiber: 6 g

NOTES

RATING

DIFFICULTY

Caesar Salad

PREP 20 MIN

COOK 0 MIN

4 SERVES

Ingredients & Tools

Salad:

- 2 heads of Romaine lettuce, washed and chopped
- 1 cup croutons, preferably homemade
- 1/2 cup grated Parmesan cheese
- 1/4 cup shaved Parmesan cheese (for garnish)
- 2 anchovy fillets, finely chopped (optional)

Dressing:

- 1 clove garlic, minced
- 2 tablespoons fresh lemon juice
- 1 teaspoon Dijon mustard
- 1 teaspoon Worcestershire sauce
- 1 small egg yolk (or 1 tablespoon mayonnaise for a raw egg-free version)
- 1/3 cup extra virgin olive oil
- Salt and black pepper to taste

Tips for Success

Fresh Ingredients: Use fresh Romaine lettuce for the best texture and flavor.

Dressing Consistency: If the dressing is too thick, thin it with a little water or more lemon juice.

Egg Yolk Caution: If using raw egg yolk in the dressing, ensure it's from a trusted source to minimize the risk of salmonella. Alternatively, use mayonnaise as a safer option.

It is recommended to opt for whole grain croutons to increase fiber content and nutritional value. For extra flavor, make homemade croutons by tossing cubed bread with olive oil, garlic powder, and salt, then baking until golden.

METHOD

Step 1: Prepare the Dressing:
In a small bowl, whisk together the garlic, lemon juice, Dijon mustard, Worcestershire sauce, and egg yolk. Gradually whisk in the olive oil until the dressing is emulsified. Season with salt and pepper to taste.

Step 2:
In a large bowl, toss the chopped Romaine lettuce with the croutons, grated Parmesan, and anchovies if using.

Step 3:
Drizzle with the prepared dressing and toss until all the ingredients are well coated.
Garnish with shaved Parmesan cheese and serve immediately.

Per Serving:

- **Calories:** 300 kcal
- **Protein:** 8 g
- **Fat:** 25 g

Carbohydrates: 12 g
Fiber: 3 g

NOTES

RATING

DIFFICULTY

BLT Sandwich (Bacon, Lettuce, Tomato)

PREP 10 MIN

COOK 10 MIN

1 SERVE

Benefits of BLT Sandwich

Whole Grain Bread: Rich in fiber and B vitamins

aids digestion,

supports energy metabolism.

Bacon: Provides protein and B vitamins

for muscle growth and repair.

Lettuce: Low in calories and contains fiber, vitamin C, and potassium

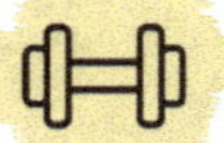
to stay fit and healthy.

Ingredients & Tools

- 4 slices of bacon
- 2 slices of whole grain bread
- 2-3 leaves of romaine lettuce or iceberg lettuce
- 2 slices of ripe tomato
- 1 tablespoon mayonnaise (optional)
- Salt and pepper to taste

Dressing:

- 1 clove garlic, minced
- 2 tablespoons fresh lemon juice
- 1 teaspoon Dijon mustard
- 1 teaspoon Worcestershire sauce
- 1 small egg yolk (or 1 tablespoon mayonnaise for a raw egg-free version)
- 1/3 cup extra virgin olive oil
- Salt and black pepper to taste

Tips for Success

- **Crisp the Bacon Well:** Crisp bacon adds a satisfying crunch and flavor.
- **Use Fresh Ingredients:** Fresh, crisp lettuce and ripe tomatoes enhance the texture and taste.
- **Toast the Bread:** Toasting adds crunch and prevents the bread from getting soggy.

It is recommended to limit your daily bread consumption to ensure you're not overloading on simple carbohydrates, which can contribute to weight gain and fluctuations in blood sugar levels. Look for bacon with fewer additives and artificial ingredients. More natural ingredients usually indicate a better quality.

METHOD

Step 1: Cook the Bacon:
Heat a skillet over medium heat. Add bacon slices and cook until crisp, about 3-5 minutes per side. Remove and place on paper towels to drain excess fat.

Step 2:
Toast the bread slices lightly if desired.
Spread mayonnaise on one side of each bread slice.

Step 3: Place lettuce leaves on one slice of bread, top with tomato slices, season with a pinch of salt and pepper, and add the cooked bacon.
Top with the second slice of bread, mayo side down.

Step 4: Serve:
Cut the sandwiches in half if desired and serve immediately. Pair the sandwich with a side of fruit or yogurt to make it a balanced meal suitable for a teen's dietary needs.

Per Serving:

- Calories: 350-400
- Protein: 15-20g
- Fat: 20-25g

Carbohydrates: 30-35g
Fiber: 5-6g
Sodium: 500-600mg

NOTES

RATING

DIFFICULTY

Cheese Quesadilla

PREP 5 MIN

COOK 10 MIN

2 SERVES

Benefits of Cheese Quesadilla

Whole Wheat Tortillas: Higher in fiber than white tortillas

aid digestion.

Bell Peppers and Onions: Provide vitamins A and C

to have healthy skin, hair, and nails.

Cheese: Good source of calcium and protein

for muscle growth and repair,

for strong bones and teeth.

Ingredients & Tools

- 2 large whole wheat tortillas
- 1 cup shredded cheese (mix of cheddar and Monterey Jack)
- 1/2 cup diced bell peppers (optional)
- 1/2 cup chopped onions (optional)
- 2 teaspoons olive oil or butter
- Salsa, sour cream, or guacamole for serving

Tips for Success

Use a Combination of Cheeses: A mix of cheddar and Monterey Jack offers a good melt with a rich flavor.

Don't Overstuff: Keep fillings balanced so they heat through evenly and the quesadilla is easy to flip.

Cook on Medium Heat: Ensures that the tortilla crisps without burning and the cheese melts perfectly.

It is recommended that you limit your quesadilla consumption. While delicious, quesadillas should be enjoyed in moderation due to their high cheese content, which can be high in saturated fat. Some cheeses can be high in sodium. Look for low-sodium versions of your favorite cheeses to help manage your salt intake. Opt for cheeses like mozzarella, ricotta, or feta, which are lower in fat than cream cheese or cheddar.

METHOD

Step 1: Prepare the Fillings:
Heat one teaspoon of oil in a skillet over medium heat. Sauté onions and bell peppers until soft, about 3-5 minutes. Set aside.

Step 2: Assemble the Quesadilla:
Lay one tortilla flat on a plate. Sprinkle half the cheese on the tortilla, add the sautéed onions and bell peppers, then sprinkle the remaining cheese. Top with the second tortilla.

Step 3: Cook the Quesadilla:
Heat the remaining oil or butter in the skillet over medium heat. Carefully place the assembled quesadilla in the skillet. Cook for about 2-3 minutes on each side or until the tortillas are golden brown and the cheese is melted.

Step 4: Serve:
Remove from the skillet and let sit for a minute. Cut into wedges and serve with salsa, sour cream, or guacamole. Pair your quesadilla with a side of salad or a piece of fruit to balance out the meal.

Per Serving:

- **Calories:** 400-450
- **Protein:** 18-22g
- **Fat:** 20-25g
- **Carbohydrates:** 35-40g
- **Fiber:** 5-6g
- **Sodium:** 600-700mg

NOTES

RATING

DIFFICULTY

Macaroni and Cheese

PREP 10 MIN

COOK 20 MIN

4 SERVES

Benefits of Macaroni and Cheese

Whole Grain Pasta: Opting for whole grain macaroni increases fiber content,

which aids digestion.

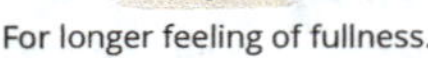

For longer feeling of fullness.

Whole Milk and Cheese: Provides calcium and vitamin D

for muscle growth and repair.

For strong bones and teeth.

Ingredients & Tools

- 8 oz (about 2 cups) elbow macaroni
- 2 tablespoons butter
- 2 tablespoons all-purpose flour
- 2 cups milk (preferably whole or 2%)
- 1/2 teaspoon salt
- 1/4 teaspoon black pepper
- 1/4 teaspoon paprika (optional)
- 2 cups shredded sharp cheddar cheese
- 1/2 cup grated Parmesan cheese

Tips for Success

- **Cheese Quality:** Use good quality cheese as it's the main flavor component. Grate your own cheese for better melting.
- **Sauce Consistency:** Be patient when making the sauce; a slow and steady whisk will help achieve a smooth consistency.
- **Pasta Doneness:** Cook your pasta al dente as it will continue to cook in the oven.

It is recommended to enjoy macaroni in moderation as part of a balanced diet because it is rich in dairy and carbohydrates. Serve with a side salad or steamed vegetables to add nutrients and fiber to your meal. Add cooked vegetables like broccoli or diced tomatoes to the dish to increase its nutritional value and add flavor.

METHOD

Step 1: Cook the Macaroni: Bring a large pot of salted water to a boil. Add the macaroni and cook until al dente, about 8 minutes. Drain and set aside.

Step 2: Make the Cheese Sauce:
In the same pot, melt butter over medium heat. Stir in flour and cook for about 1 minute to remove the raw flour taste. Gradually whisk in milk, ensuring there are no lumps. Add salt, pepper, and paprika.

Step 3: Cook the mixture, stirring constantly, until it thickens and begins to bubble, about 5-6 minutes, about 5-6 minutes.
Reduce heat to low and stir in shredded cheddar and Parmesan cheese until melted and smooth.

Step 4: Combine and Bake:
Preheat the oven to 350°F (175°C).
Combine the cooked macaroni with the cheese sauce, mixing well. Transfer to a greased baking dish.
(Optional) For a crunchy topping, sprinkle with breadcrumbs and a few pats of butter.
Bake in the preheated oven for 15-20 minutes until bubbly and golden on top.

Per Serving:

- Calories: 500-550
- Protein: 25-30g
- Fat: 25-30g

Carbohydrates: 50-55g
Fiber: 2-3g
Sodium: 700-750mg

NOTES

RATING

DIFFICULTY

Basic Sushi Roll

PREP 30 MIN

COOK 20 MIN

4 SERVES

Benefits of Sushi Roll

Sushi Rice: Provides carbohydrates

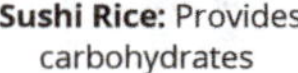

aids digestion,

for energy.

Nori: Rich in iodine, which is crucial for thyroid function, and also provides vitamins A, C, and E

to stay healthy.

Cucumber and Avocado: Provide fiber, vitamins, and healthy fats. **Sushi-grade Fish**: Excellent source of high-quality protein and omega-3 fatty acids

promote heart health.

To stay smart

Ingredients & Tools

- 2 cups sushi rice
- 2 1/2 cups water
- 1/3 cup rice vinegar
- 2 tablespoons sugar
- 1 teaspoon salt
- 4 sheets of nori (seaweed)
- 1 small cucumber, julienned
- 1 avocado, sliced
- 8 ounces of sushi-grade tuna or salmon, sliced into strips
- Soy sauce, wasabi, and pickled ginger for serving

Tips for Success

- **Rice Preparation:** Make sure the rice is seasoned well and cooled slightly before spreading on the nori. This helps the sushi to roll easily and taste authentic.
- **Keep Ingredients Fresh:** Use the freshest ingredients for the best flavor and texture, especially the fish, which must be sushi-grade for safe raw consumption.

It is recommended to consume condiments in moderation. Soy sauce is high in sodium, and wasabi can be very spicy. Pair your sushi with a light soup, such as miso soup, to round out your meal with additional nutrients and hydration.

METHOD

Step 1: Rinse the sushi rice under cold water until the water runs clear. Add to a rice cooker or a pot with 2 1/2 cups of water and cook according to the rice cooker's instructions. If cooking in a pot, once boiling, reduce the heat to the lowest setting, cover the pot, and let it simmer for 18-20 minutes. Do not lift the lid during this time as the steam cooks the rice. After 20 minutes, remove the pot from heat and let it sit, still covered, for 10 minutes. This allows the rice to finish steaming and become fluffy.

Step 2: While the rice is cooking, mix rice vinegar, sugar, and salt in a small bowl until dissolved.

Transfer the cooked rice to a large wooden or plastic bowl (avoid metal as it reacts with the vinegar). Gently fold in the vinegar mixture with a rice paddle or wooden spoon. Cover with a damp cloth until ready to use.

Step 3: Assemble the Sushi Rolls:

Place a sheet of nori on a bamboo sushi mat. With wet hands, spread about 1/2 cup of sushi rice evenly over the nori, leaving about 2 inches of space at the top.

Lay strips of cucumber, avocado, and fish along the bottom edge of the rice-covered nori.

Begin rolling the nori tightly from the bottom using the mat to keep the roll tight. Use a little water to seal the edge of the nori.

Step 4: Cut and Serve:

With a sharp, wet knife, cut the roll into 6-8 pieces. A sharp knife is crucial for cutting sushi rolls cleanly. Wetting the knife prevents rice from sticking and ensures smooth cuts. Clean the knife after each cut to ensure a clean slice.

Serve with soy sauce, wasabi, and pickled ginger.

Per Serving:

- Calories: 300-350
- Protein: 10-15g
- Fat: 9-12g
- Carbohydrates: 45-50g
- Fiber: 3-4g
- Sodium: 300-400mg

NOTES

RATING

DIFFICULTY

Spaghetti with Marinara Sauce

PREP 10 MIN

COOK 20 MIN

4 SERVES

Benefits of Spaghetti with Marinara Sauce

Whole Wheat Spaghetti: Higher in fiber than regular spaghetti

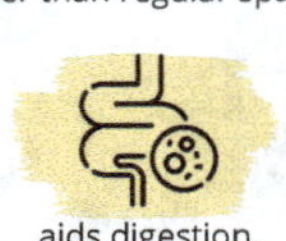

aids digestion.

Longer feeling of fullness.

Garlic and Onions: Offer anti-inflammatory benefits

to boost the immune system.

Tomatoes: High in vitamin C and lycopene, an antioxidant. **Olive Oil:** Contains monounsaturated fats

promote heart health.

Ingredients & Tools

- 12 oz spaghetti (whole wheat recommended for added fiber)
- 2 tablespoons olive oil
- 1 onion, finely chopped
- 2 garlic cloves, minced
- 1 can (28 ounces) crushed tomatoes
- 1 teaspoon dried basil
- 1 teaspoon dried oregano
- 1/2 teaspoon salt
- 1/4 teaspoon black pepper
- Fresh basil leaves (optional, for garnish)
- Grated Parmesan cheese (optional, for serving)

Tips for Success

- **Pasta Water:** Save some of the water in which you cooked the pasta. Its starch content is great for adjusting the consistency of your sauce.
- **Simmering the Sauce:** Allow the marinara sauce to simmer for at least 15 minutes to develop depth of flavor.
- **Fresh Ingredients:** Using fresh basil and real Parmesan cheese for garnish can significantly enhance the flavor of the dish.

It is recommended to watch portion sizes, especially if watching calorie intake, as pasta dishes can be quite filling. Pair the spaghetti with a side salad dressed with a vinaigrette to incorporate more vegetables into your meal.

METHOD

Step 1: Cook the Spaghetti:
Bring a large pot of salted water to a boil. Add the spaghetti and cook according to package instructions for al dente. Drain and set aside, reserving 1 cup of pasta water to adjust the sauce consistency later if needed.

Step 2: Make the Marinara Sauce:
In a large skillet or saucepan, heat the olive oil over medium heat. Add the chopped onion and cook until translucent, about 5 minutes.
Add the minced garlic and cook for another minute until fragrant.
Stir in the crushed tomatoes, dried basil, oregano, salt, and pepper. Bring to a simmer and let cook for 15-20 minutes to allow the flavors to meld together.

Step 3: Add the minced garlic and cook for another minute until fragrant.
Stir in the crushed tomatoes, dried basil, oregano, salt, and pepper. Bring to a simmer and let cook for 15-20 minutes to allow the flavors to meld together. meld together.

Step 4: Combine and Serve:
Toss the cooked spaghetti with the marinara sauce, adding a little reserved pasta water if the sauce needs thinning.
Serve hot, garnished with fresh basil leaves and grated Parmesan cheese if desired.

Per Serving:

- Calories: 330-380
- Protein: 10-12g
- Fat: 7-9g
- Carbohydrates: 60-65g
- Fiber: 6-8g
- Sodium: 300-400mg

NOTES

RATING

DIFFICULTY

Chicken Caesar Wrap

PREP 10 MIN

COOK 0 MIN
(if using pre-cooked chicken)

4 SERVES

Benefits of Chicken Caesar Wrap

Whole Wheat Tortillas: Higher in fiber than white tortillas

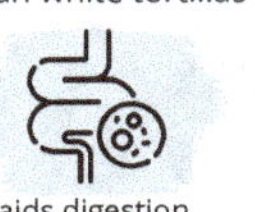

aids digestion,

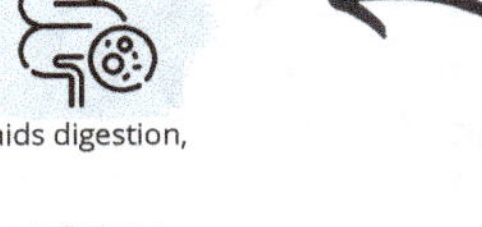

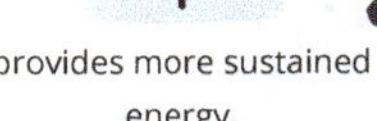

provides more sustained energy.

Chicken: A great source of lean protein. **Parmesan Cheese** offers calcium and protein, important for bone health.

For muscle growth and repair

Romaine Lettuce: Low in calories and high in dietary fiber, vitamins C and K.

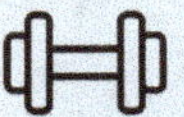

To stay fit and healthy.

Ingredients & Tools

- 2 cups cooked chicken (preferably grilled or roasted)
- 4 large whole wheat tortillas
- 1 cup chopped romaine lettuce
- 1/2 cup grated Parmesan cheese
- 1/2 cup Caesar dressing
- 1/4 cup croutons, lightly crushed (optional for added crunch)
- Black pepper to taste

Tips for Success

- **Balance the Dressing:** Use enough dressing to flavor the wrap without making it soggy.
- **Secure the Wrap:** A tight roll is essential to keep all the ingredients contained. Tucking in the ends as you roll helps.
- **Variations:** Customize the wrap with additional ingredients like sliced tomatoes, onions, or cucumbers for extra nutrition and flavor.

It is recommended to be mindful of the Caesar dressing amount used to keep the wrap healthier, as it is rich and can be high in calories.

METHOD

Step 1: Prepare the Ingredients:
If you don't have pre-cooked chicken, grill or roast chicken breasts seasoned with a little salt and pepper. To cook chicken on a stove, place the skillet on medium heat and add the olive oil or butter. Allow it to heat up. Carefully place the chicken breasts in the hot skillet. Let them cook undisturbed for about 5-7 minutes on the first side. You're looking for a golden-brown crust to form. Using tongs, flip the chicken breasts to the other side. Cook for another 5-7 minutes. Wait until it is cooled, and cut the chicken breast into small pieces.

Step 2: Wash and chop the romaine lettuce. Grate the Parmesan cheese if not pre-grated.

Step 3: Assemble the Wraps:
Lay a whole wheat tortilla flat on a clean surface.
Spread about 2 tablespoons of Caesar dressing over the tortilla.
Add a layer of romaine lettuce, then sprinkle a quarter of the chicken and Parmesan cheese on top.
Add crushed croutons if using for extra crunch.
Season with a little black pepper.

Step 4: Roll the Wrap:
Fold the bottom of the tortilla over the filling. Fold in the sides and then roll tightly to enclose the filling completely. The wrap can be eaten immediately or wrapped in foil to take on the go. It can also be sliced in half to make it easier to eat.

Per Serving:

- Calories: 400-450
- Protein: 25-30g
- Fat: 20-25g
- Carbohydrates: 30-35g
- Fiber: 4-5g
- Sodium: 700-800mg

NOTES

RATING

DIFFICULTY

Meatball Sandwich

PREP 20 MIN

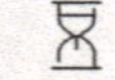
COOK 30 MIN

4 SERVES

Benefits of Meatball Sandwich

Marinara Sauce: Contains tomatoes, which are high in vitamin C and lycopene, antioxidants

promote heart health.

For flawless skin.

Whole Wheat Buns: (if using) Offers more fiber than white buns

provides more sustained energy.

Ground Beef: Good source of protein and iron.

For muscle growth and repair.

Parmesan Cheese: Provides calcium.

For strong bones and teeth.

Ingredients & Tools

For the Meatballs:

1 pound ground beef (or mix of beef and pork)
1/4 cup breadcrumbs
1/4 cup grated Parmesan cheese
1 large egg
2 cloves garlic, minced
1 teaspoon dried oregano
1/2 teaspoon salt
1/2 teaspoon black pepper

For the Sandwich:

4 hoagie rolls or sub buns
1 cup marinara sauce (store-bought or homemade)
1 cup shredded mozzarella cheese
Fresh basil leaves (optional for garnish)

Tips for Success

- **Browning Meatballs:** Browning the meatballs before simmering them in the sauce adds flavor and texture.
- **Cheese Options:** You can also use slices of provolone or fresh mozzarella for a different taste and texture.

It is recommended to pair your meatball sandwich with a side salad or steamed vegetables to incorporate more fiber and vitamins into your meal.

METHOD

Step 1: Make the Meatballs:
In a large bowl, combine the ground meat, breadcrumbs, Parmesan cheese, egg, minced garlic, oregano, salt, and pepper. Mix well until everything is evenly distributed. Make sure the meatball mixture isn't too wet or dry. Adjust breadcrumbs or add a little milk if needed.

Step 2: In a skillet over medium heat, brown the meatballs on all sides, then add the marinara sauce. Cover and simmer for 20 minutes until the meatballs are cooked through.

Step 3: Prepare the Sandwich:
Preheat your oven to 350°F (175°C).
Split the hoagie rolls or sub-buns without cutting through completely.
Place an equal number of meatballs in each bun.
Spoon extra marinara sauce over the meatballs.
Sprinkle shredded mozzarella cheese over the top.

Step 4: Bake the Sandwich:
Place the prepared sandwiches on a baking sheet and bake in the preheated oven for 10 minutes or until the cheese is melted and bubbly and the buns are toasty. Garnish with fresh basil leaves if desired. Serve hot.

Per Serving:

- Calories: 650-700
- Protein: 35-40g
- Fat: 30-35g
- Carbohydrates: 55-60g
- Fiber: 4-5g
- Sodium: 900-1000mg

NOTES

RATING

DIFFICULTY

Pulled Pork Sandwich

PREP 15 MIN

COOK 30 MIN

4 SERVES

Benefits of Pulled Pork Sandwich

Coleslaw: If made with a vinegar-based dressing, provides a good source of vitamin C and K from the cabbage.

For flawless skin.

Boost the immune system.

Pork Shoulder: Rich in protein

For muscle growth and repair.

Whole Wheat Buns: (if using) Offers more fiber than white buns

provides more sustained energy.

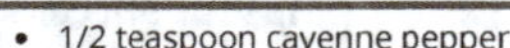

Ingredients & Tools

For the Pulled Pork:

- 3-4 pounds pork shoulder (also known as pork butt)
- 2 tablespoons brown sugar
- 1 tablespoon paprika
- 1 tablespoon salt
- 1 teaspoon black pepper
- 1 teaspoon garlic powder
- 1 teaspoon onion powder
- 1/2 teaspoon cayenne pepper
- 1 cup apple cider vinegar
- 1 cup water
- 2 tablespoons Worcestershire sauce
- **For the Sandwich:**
- 6-8 hamburger buns, preferably whole wheat
- BBQ sauce
- Coleslaw

Tips for Success

Generous Seasoning: Don't skimp on the seasoning. A good rub not only adds flavor but also helps to create a delicious crust on the meat, especially when searing.

Skillet Cooking: Manage your heat effectively. Start with a high heat to sear the meat and develop flavors, then lower it to simmer gently, allowing the meat to cook through without drying out.

It is recommended to keep your portion sizes in check can help manage calorie intake and maintain a balanced diet. Pulled pork is rich and flavorful, but it can also be high in calories and fats, especially saturated fats.

METHOD

Step 1:
Instead of using a whole pork shoulder, purchase pork tenderloin or loin cuts, which are leaner and cook faster. Slice them into thin strips or small chunks. Season the pork pieces with the spice rub.

Step 2: Heat a large skillet over medium-high heat and add a bit of oil. Sear the pork pieces until they are browned on all sides, then reduce the heat. Add a small amount the original mixture of vinegar and Worcestershire sauce to the pan, cover, and let simmer for about 20-25 minutes until the pork is tender enough to shred. Once cooked and tender, shred the pork directly in the skillet using forks.

Step 3: Once cooked and tender, shred the pork directly in the skillet using forks. For the best texture, use two forks to pull the meat apart. This method helps to preserve the fibrous texture of the pork, which is key to a good pulled pork.

Step 4: Assemble the Sandwich:
Toast the hamburger buns lightly if desired. Pile a generous amount of pulled pork onto each bun. Top with BBQ sauce and coleslaw if using. Serve the sandwiches hot, with extra BBQ sauce on the side if preferred.

Per Serving:

- Calories: 600-650
- Protein: 40-45g
- Fat: 25-30g
- Carbohydrates: 55-60g
- Fiber: 3-4g
- Sodium: 800-900mg

NOTES

RATING

DIFFICULTY

Veggie Burger

PREP 20 MIN

COOK 10 MIN

4 SERVES

Benefits of Veggie Burger

Black Beans: High in protein and fiber

for muscle growth and repair.

Whole Grains: Using breadcrumbs made from whole grains add fiber and nutrients.

Provides more sustained energy.

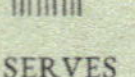

Vegetables: Carrots, onions, and bell peppers are high in vitamins and antioxidants.

Boost the immune system.

For growth .

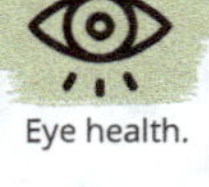

Eye health.

Ingredients & Tools

For the Burger Patties:

- 1 can (15 oz) black beans, drained and rinsed
- 1/2 cup breadcrumbs
- 1/4 cup grated carrot
- 1/4 cup finely chopped onion
- 2 cloves garlic, minced
- 1 small green bell pepper, finely chopped
- 1 large egg (or for vegan option: 1 tbsp flaxseed meal mixed with 3 tbsp water)
- 1 teaspoon cumin
- 1/2 teaspoon salt
- 1/2 teaspoon pepper
- 2 tablespoons olive oil for cooking

For Assembly:

- Whole wheat burger buns
- Lettuce leaves
- Sliced tomato
- Sliced avocado
- Your choice of sauce (e.g., ketchup, mustard, vegan mayo)

Tips for Success

Binding the Patties: If the mixture feels too wet or crumbly, adjust the consistency with more breadcrumbs or a bit more flaxseed meal to help the patties hold together better.

Flavor Variations: Experiment with different spices and herbs like paprika, coriander, or fresh parsley to vary the flavor profile of your burgers.

It is recommended to be mindful of the sodium content in canned beans and breadcrumbs. Opt for low-sodium or no-salt-added versions of ingredients whenever possible. Limit your daily bread consumption to ensure you're not overloading on simple carbohydrates, opt for whole-wheat buns.

METHOD

Step 1: In a bowl, mash the black beans until mostly smooth but still a bit chunky for texture.

Stir in the breadcrumbs, grated carrot, chopped onion, minced garlic, green pepper, egg (or flaxseed mixture), cumin, salt, and pepper. Mix until well combined.

Form the mixture into four equal-sized patties.

Step 2: Cook the Patties:

Heat the olive oil in a non-stick skillet over medium heat. Cook the patties for about 5 minutes on each side or until they are golden and firm.

Step 3: Prepare the whole wheat buns:

Cut the buns in half. Toast the whole wheat buns lightly.

Step 4: Place a lettuce leaf on the bottom half of each bun, followed by the veggie patty. Top with sliced tomato, avocado, and your choice of sauce. Cover with the top half of the bun and serve.

Per Serving:

- Calories: 200-250
- Protein: 8-10g
- Fat: 7-9g
- Carbohydrates: 30-35g
- Fiber: 6-8g
- Sodium: 300-400mg

NOTES

RATING

DIFFICULTY

Pasta Salad

PREP 20 MIN

COOK 10 MIN

4 SERVES

Benefits of Pasta Salad

Olives and Olive Oil: Rich in monounsaturated fats.

For muscle growth and repair.

Whole Wheat Pasta: Higher in fiber and nutrients compared to regular pasta.

Provides more sustained energy.

Vegetables: A great source of vitamins, minerals, and antioxidants. Bell peppers and tomatoes are high in vitamin C.

Boost the immune system.

Feta Cheese: Provides calcium and protein but is lower in fat and calories than many other cheeses.

For strong bones and teeth.

Ingredients & Tools

- **For the Pasta Salad:**
  - 8 oz whole wheat pasta (penne, fusilli, or rotini work well)
  - 1 cup cherry tomatoes, halved
  - 1 cucumber, diced
  - 1 red bell pepper, diced
  - 1/2 red onion, thinly sliced
  - 1/4 cup sliced black olives
  - 1/4 cup crumbled feta cheese
  - 1/4 cup fresh basil leaves, chopped

For the Dressing:

- 1/4 cup olive oil
- 2 tablespoons red wine vinegar
- 1 teaspoon Dijon mustard
- 1 garlic clove, minced
- Salt and pepper to taste

Tips for Success

Pasta Choice: Use pasta shapes that have holes or ridges as they hold the dressing better.

Fresh Ingredients: Use fresh, crisp vegetables for the best texture and flavor.

Adjust to Taste: Feel free to adjust the amount of each vegetable or the dressing ingredients to suit your taste. Adding proteins like grilled chicken can turn this side dish into a hearty main.

It is recommended to add a protein source like grilled chicken, tuna, or chickpeas to make it more filling. Pasta is relatively high in calories and carbohydrates. Consuming large portions can contribute to calorie excess, which may lead to weight gain if not balanced with physical activity.

METHOD

Step 1: Cook the Pasta:
Bring a large pot of salted water to a boil. Add the pasta and cook according to the package instructions until al dente. Drain and rinse under cold water to cool.

Step 2: Prepare the Vegetables:
While the pasta is cooking, prepare the tomatoes, cucumber, bell pepper, and red onion.

Step 3: Make the Dressing:
In a small bowl, whisk together olive oil, red wine vinegar, Dijon mustard, minced garlic, salt, and pepper until well combined.

Step 4: In a large bowl, combine the cooled pasta, prepared vegetables, sliced olives, and crumbled feta cheese. Pour the dressing over the salad and toss to coat evenly. Sprinkle chopped basil over the top. Allow the salad to chill in the refrigerator for at least 30 minutes before serving.

Per Serving:

- Calories: 300-350
- Protein: 8-10g
- Fat: 15-18g
- Carbohydrates: 35-40g
- Fiber: 5-6g
- Sodium: 200-250mg

NOTES

RATING

DIFFICULTY

Chicken Tenders

PREP 15 MIN

COOK 20 MIN

4 SERVES

Benefits of Chicken Tenders

Chicken Breast: A lean source of high-quality protein

for muscle growth and repair.

Whole Wheat Breadcrumbs: Provide more fiber than regular breadcrumbs

for prolonged satiety.

Greek Yogurt: Used in the dipping sauce, it provides additional protein and probiotics

aids digestion.

Parmesan Cheese: Adds calcium

for strong bones and teeth.

Ingredients & Tools

- **For the Chicken Tenders:**
- 1 pound boneless, skinless chicken breasts, cut into strips
- 1 cup buttermilk (or 1 cup milk mixed with 1 tablespoon lemon juice or vinegar)
- 1 cup whole wheat breadcrumbs
- 1/2 cup grated Parmesan cheese
- 1 teaspoon paprika
    - 1 teaspoon garlic powder
    - 1/2 teaspoon salt
    - 1/2 teaspoon black pepper
    - Olive oil spray (or a light drizzle of olive oil)
- **For Dipping Sauce:**
    - 1/2 cup Greek yogurt
    - 1 tablespoon honey
    - 1 tablespoon mustard
    - Salt and pepper to taste

Tips for Success

Buttermilk Substitute: If you don't have buttermilk, you can easily make it by mixing milk with a tablespoon of lemon juice or vinegar. Let it sit for 5 minutes before using.

Ensure Crispiness: The olive oil helps the breadcrumbs turn golden and crispy in the oven, mimicking the fried texture without the need for deep frying.

Paprika Variation: You can use smoked paprika for a slightly smoky flavor.

It is recommended to serve these chicken tenders with a side of steamed vegetables or a fresh salad to round out the meal with fiber and essential nutrients.

METHOD

Step 1: Marinate the Chicken:

Place the chicken strips in a bowl and cover with buttermilk. Let them marinate in the refrigerator for at least 1 hour or overnight to tenderize the meat and enhance flavor. In another bowl, mix the whole wheat breadcrumbs, grated Parmesan, paprika, garlic powder, salt, and pepper.

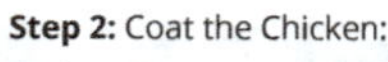

Step 2: Coat the Chicken:

Preheat your oven to 425°F (220°C). Line a baking sheet with parchment paper.

Remove a chicken strip from the buttermilk, let the excess drip off, then dredge in the breadcrumb mixture, pressing to coat thoroughly.

Place the coated chicken strips on the prepared baking sheet. Repeat with all chicken strips.

Spray lightly with olive oil spray or drizzle with a little olive oil.

Step 3: Bake in the preheated oven for 10 minutes. Flip each piece and continue baking for another 10 minutes or until the chicken is golden brown and cooked through.

Step 4: Prepare the Dipping Sauce:

While the chicken is baking, mix Greek yogurt, honey, mustard, salt, and pepper in a small bowl. Adjust seasoning to taste.

Serve the chicken tenders hot with the dipping sauce on the side.

Per Serving:

- Calories: 300-350
- Protein: 28-32g
- Fat: 8-10g
- Carbohydrates: 20-25g
- Fiber: 2-3g
- Sodium: 400-450mg

NOTES

RATING

DIFFICULTY

Philly Cheesesteak

PREP 10 MIN

COOK 20 MIN

4 SERVES

Benefits of Philly Cheesesteak

Ribeye Steak: Provides a high-quality source of protein and important nutrients like iron and B vitamins

to stay fit and healthy.

For energy metabolism.

Olive Oil: A healthier fat option

Promote heart health.

Onion: Contains antioxidants and compounds.

Help reduce inflammation.

Ingredients & Tools

- 1 lb ribeye steak, thinly sliced
- 1 large onion, thinly sliced
- 2 tablespoons olive oil
- 4 hoagie rolls, split
- 8 slices of provolone cheese
- Salt and pepper to taste
- Optional: sliced mushrooms, bell peppers

Tips for Success

Meat Selection: Ribeye is traditional for its flavor and tenderness, but you can also use top sirloin for a leaner option.

Cheese Options: Provolone is traditional, but American cheese or Cheez Whiz are also popular choices in different Philly regions.

It is recommended to limit your daily bread consumption to ensure you're not overloading on simple carbohydrates. Given the high sodium content from the cheese and possibly the meat is also recommended to consume this dish in moderation. Complement the cheesesteak with a vegetable side, like a salad or steamed vegetables, to balance out the meal.

METHOD

Step 1: Freeze the ribeye steak for about an hour before slicing to make it easier to cut thinly. Ensure the meat is very thinly sliced to maintain authenticity and ensure it cooks quickly and evenly. Thinly slice the onion and, if using, mushrooms and bell peppers.

Step 2: Cook Vegetables:
Heat 1 tablespoon of olive oil in a large skillet over medium-high heat. Add the onions (and mushrooms and bell peppers if using) and cook until softened and caramelized, about 6-8 minutes. Remove from the skillet and set aside.

Step 2: Add the remaining tablespoon of olive oil to the skillet. Add the thinly sliced steak and season with salt and pepper. Cook, stirring frequently, until the meat is browned and no longer pink, about 3-5 minutes.

Step 3: Divide the cooked meat among the hoagie rolls. Distribute the onions and other vegetables if used over the meat. Place two slices of provolone cheese over the top of the meat and vegetables in each roll. Cover the skillet for a minute with a lid to melt the cheese with the residual heat. Serve the sandwiches hot.

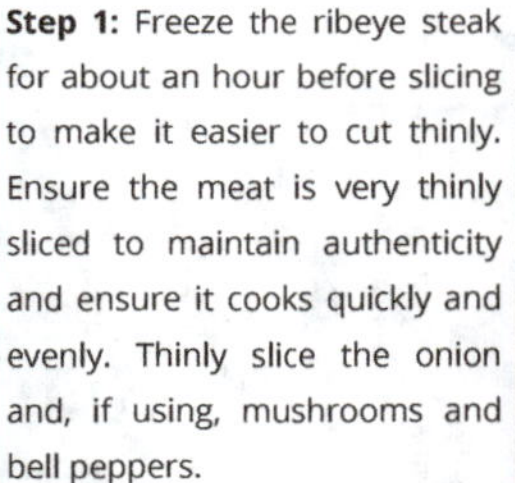

Per Serving:

- Calories: 600-650
- Protein: 40-45g
- Fat: 35-40g
- Carbohydrates: 40-45g
- Fiber: 2-3g
- Sodium: 800-1000mg

NOTES

RATING

DIFFICULTY

Pita Pocket with Hummus and Veggies

PREP 15 MIN

COOK 0 MIN

2 SERVES

Benefits of Pita Pocket with Hummus and Veggies

Feta Cheese and Olives: Provide calcium and healthy fats

For strong bones and teeth.

Whole Wheat Pita: Higher in fiber than white pita

For prolonged satiety.

Hummus: Made from chickpeas, tahini, olive oil, and lemon, it's rich in protein, healthy fats, and fiber.

Promotes heart health.

Vegetables: Cucumbers, tomatoes, bell peppers, and onions are high in vitamins, minerals, and antioxidants.

Boost the immune system

Ingredients & Tools

- **For the Pita Pocket:**
- 2 whole wheat pita breads
- 1 cup hummus (store-bought or homemade)
- 1 cucumber, sliced
- 1 tomato, sliced
- 1 bell pepper (any color), sliced
- 1 bell pepper (any color), sliced
- 1 small red onion, thinly sliced
- 1/4 cup feta cheese, crumbled (optional)
- 1/4 cup Kalamata olives, pitted and sliced (optional)
- Fresh parsley or cilantro for garnish

Tips for Success

Warm the Pita: Before assembling, you can lightly toast the pita bread to make it more pliable and easier to open without tearing.

Variety of Veggies: Feel free to add other vegetables like spinach, shredded carrots, or sprouts for extra nutrition and flavor.

Homemade Hummus: For an even healthier option, consider making your own hummus. It allows you to control the ingredients and avoid preservatives found in many store-bought versions.

This pita pocket is a balanced meal on its own, providing a good mix of macronutrients and essential vitamins and minerals. Pair this meal with a glass of water or herbal tea to aid digestion and hydration.

METHOD

Step 1: Prepare the Veggies: Wash and slice the cucumber, tomato, bell pepper, and red onion. Set aside.

Step 2: Assemble the Pita Pockets: Cut the pita breads in half to make pockets. Carefully open each half to create a space for the fillings.

Spread a generous amount of hummus inside each pita half.

Step 3: Stuff the sliced vegetables into the pita pockets. Add crumbled feta cheese and sliced olives if using.

Garnish with fresh parsley or cilantro.

Step 4: Serve the pita pockets immediately, or wrap them in foil or parchment paper for an on-the-go meal.

Per Serving:

- Calories: 300-350
- Protein: 10-12g
- Fat: 15-18g
- Carbohydrates: 35-40g
- Fiber: 6-8g
- Sodium: 300-400mg

NOTES

RATING

DIFFICULTY

Tuna Salad Sandwich

PREP 15 MIN | COOK 0 MIN | 2 SERVES

Benefits of Tuna Salad Sandwich

Tuna: High in protein and rich in omega-3 fatty acids.

Promote heart health.

Whole Grain Bread: Provides fiber.

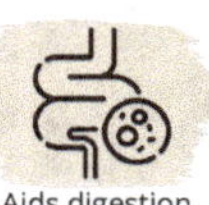

Aids digestion.

Celery and Cucumber: Low in calories and high in water content.

Hydrating and good for digestion.

Onion: Contains antioxidants and compounds.

Help reduce inflammation.

Ingredients & Tools

For the Tuna Salad:

- 2 cans (5 ounces each) tuna in water, drained
- 1/4 cup mayonnaise (use light mayonnaise or yogurt for a healthier option)
- 2 celery stalks, finely chopped
- 1/4 red onion, finely chopped
- 1 tablespoon lemon juice
- 1 tablespoon Dijon mustard
- Salt and pepper to taste
- 1 tablespoon chopped fresh parsley (optional)
- **For the Sandwich:**
- 4 slices of whole grain bread, toasted
- Lettuce leaves
- Tomato slices
- Cucumber slices

Tips for Success

Lighter Mayo Alternative: Substitute mayonnaise with Greek yogurt to reduce fat content and add a boost of protein.

Enhance the Flavor: Add capers or pickles chopped finely to the tuna salad for an extra tangy flavor.

Make it Crunchy: Include sliced bell peppers or radishes for additional crunch and nutrition.

It is recommended be mindful of the sodium content, especially if using canned tuna and prepared mayonnaise. Opt for low-sodium tuna and mayo if possible. Limit your daily bread consumption to ensure you're not overloading on simple carbohydrates.

METHOD

Step 1:

In a mixing bowl, combine the drained tuna, mayonnaise, chopped celery, red onion, lemon juice, Dijon mustard, and a pinch of salt and pepper. Mix until well combined.

Stir in the chopped parsley if using for added flavor and freshness.

Step 2:

Toast the whole wheat bread lightly if desired.

Step 2:

Spread a generous amount of tuna salad on two slices of toasted whole grain bread. Layer lettuce, tomato slices, and cucumber slices over the tuna salad. Top with the remaining slices of bread.

Step 3: Serve:

Cut the sandwiches in half if desired and serve immediately, or wrap them up for a meal on the go.

Per Serving:

- Calories: 350-400
- Protein: 25-30g
- Fat: 15-20g
- Carbohydrates: 30-35g
- Fiber: 5-6g
- Sodium: 500-600mg

NOTES

RATING

DIFFICULTY

Hot Dog

PREP 10 MIN

COOK 10 MIN

4 SERVES

Benefits of Hot Dog

Turkey or Natural Sausages: Choosing turkey or sausages

to stay fit and healthy.

Whole Wheat Buns: Higher in fiber than traditional white buns

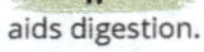

aids digestion.

Sauerkraut: Offers a good source of dietary fiber, vitamin C, and probiotics

Hydrating and good for digestion.

Onion: Contains antioxidants and compounds.

Help reduce inflammation.

Ingredients & Tools

- **For the Hot Dog:**
- 4 high-quality hot dog sausages (preferably made from all-natural ingredients or turkey for a healthier option)
- 4 whole wheat hot dog buns
- Mustard
- Ketchup
- Relish

- **Optional Toppings:**
- Sautéed onions
- Sauerkraut
- Sliced pickles
- Jalapeños (if you like it spicy)
- Shredded cheese (optional)

Tips for Success

Avoid Overcooking: Keep an eye on your cooking hot dogs to prevent them from splitting or becoming too tough.

Healthier Choices: Opt for low-sodium and sugar-free versions of condiments like ketchup and mustard.

It is recommended to enjoy hot dogs in moderation due to their fat and sodium content, especially if using traditional sausages. Complement the hot dog with sides that offer fiber and vitamins, such as a fresh salad, coleslaw, or fresh fruit.

METHOD

Step 1: Cook the Hot Dogs:

Boil: Bring a pot of water to a boil, reduce to a simmer, and add the hot dogs. Simmer for 5-6 minutes.

Grill: Preheat the grill to medium heat. Grill hot dogs, turning occasionally, until heated through and slightly charred, about 5-7 minutes.

Step 2: If desired, lightly toast the whole wheat buns on a grill or in a toaster oven.

Prepare your chosen toppings. If using onions, sauté them in a small skillet with a little oil until caramelized.

Step 2: Assemble the Hot Dogs:

Place a cooked hot dog in each bun. Add mustard, ketchup, and relish as base condiments.

Top with sautéed onions, sauerkraut, sliced pickles, jalapeños, or shredded cheese as desired.

Step 3: Serve:

Serve hot with a side of vegetable sticks, such as carrot, celery, or cucumber, to add crunch and nutrition.

Per Serving:

- Calories: 250-300
- Protein: 12-15g
- Fat: 15-18g
- Carbohydrates: 20-25g
- Fiber: 2-3g
- Sodium: 500-700mg

NOTES

RATING

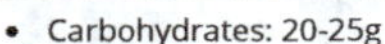

DIFFICULTY

Chicken Salad

PREP 15 MIN

COOK 0 MIN

4 SERVES

Benefits of Chicken Salad

Almonds: Rich in healthy fats, protein, and vitamin E, almonds.

Promotes heart health

Celery and Grapes: Add crunch and natural sweetness along with vitamins, minerals, and dietary fiber

to support immune system

Chicken Breast: Provides high-quality protein

For strong bones and teeth

Greek Yogurt: A healthier alternative to mayonnaise, it's lower in fat and calories and rich in protein and probiotics

Aids digestion

Ingredients & Tools

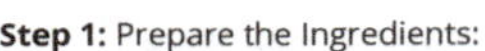

For the Chicken Salad:

- 2 cups cooked chicken breast, shredded or chopped
- 1/2 cup celery, diced
- 1/2 cup red grapes, halved
- 1/4 cup almonds, sliced or chopped
- 1/4 cup Greek yogurt (or mayonnaise for a more traditional version)
- 1 tablespoon Dijon mustard
- Salt and pepper to taste
- 1 tablespoon fresh parsley, chopped
- Optional: 1/4 cup dried cranberries for extra sweetness
- For Serving:
- Whole wheat bread, croissants, or mixed greens for a low-carb option

Tips for Success

Cooking Chicken: For extra flavor, season the chicken with herbs and spices before cooking.

Consistency: Adjust the amount of Greek yogurt based on how creamy you prefer your salad. Add a little at a time until you reach the desired consistency.

Chill Before Serving: Refrigerate the salad for at least an hour before serving to let the flavors meld together.

It is recommended to pair the chicken salad with a vegetable soup or a fresh vegetable side dish to create a balanced meal.

METHOD

Step 1: Prepare the Ingredients:
If you haven't already, cook the chicken. You can boil (10-15 minutes), grill (6-8 minutes per side), or bake (20-25 minutes, 375°F (190°C) the chicken breast, then let it cool before chopping or shredding. Dice the celery, halve the grapes, chop the almonds, and finely chop the parsley.

Step 2:
In a large bowl, combine the shredded chicken, celery, grapes, almonds, and dried cranberries (if using).
In a separate small bowl, mix the Greek yogurt and Dijon mustard together. Season with salt and pepper to taste.

Step 3: Pour the dressing over the chicken mixture and stir to combine thoroughly. Adjust seasoning if necessary. Sprinkle with fresh parsley.

Step 4: Serve the chicken salad on whole wheat bread for a sandwich, in a croissant for a rich treat, or atop a bed of mixed greens for a low-carb option.

Per Serving:

- Calories: 250-300
- Protein: 25-30g
- Fat: 10-15g
- Carbohydrates: 10-15g
- Fiber: 2-3g
- Sodium: 200-300mg

NOTES

RATING

DIFFICULTY

Sloppy Joes

PREP 10 MIN

COOK 20 MIN

4 SERVES

Benefits of Sloppy Joes

Ground Turkey: Using ground turkey instead of beef can reduce fat content

to stay fit and healthy.

Whole Wheat Buns: Higher in fiber than traditional white buns

aids digestion.

Bell Peppers and Onions: Provide a good source of vitamins C and K, fiber, and antioxidants

promote heart health.

For eye health.

Ingredients & Tools

- **For the Sloppy Joe Mix:**
- 1 lb ground beef (or turkey for a leaner option)
- 1 medium onion, finely chopped
- 1 green bell pepper, finely chopped
- 2 cloves garlic, minced
- 1 cup ketchup
- 2 tablespoons brown sugar (or honey as a natural sweetener)
- 1 tablespoon Worcestershire sauce
- 1 tablespoon mustard
- 1/2 cup water
- 1 teaspoon chili powder
- Salt and pepper to taste
- For Serving:
- 4 whole wheat hamburger buns
- Pickles or coleslaw (optional)

Tips for Success

Lean Meat: For even healthier Sloppy Joes, use ground chicken or extra lean ground turkey.

Reduce Sugar: Adjust the sweetness by reducing the amount of brown sugar or substituting it with a smaller quantity of honey.

It is recommended to limit your daily bread consumption to ensure you're not overloading on simple carbohydrates. Serve with a side salad or steamed vegetables to add fiber and nutrients, creating a balanced meal.

METHOD

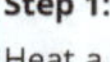

Step 1:

Heat a large skillet over medium heat. Add the ground beef (or turkey), onion, bell pepper, and garlic. Cook, stirring and breaking up the meat with a spoon, until the meat is browned and the vegetables are tender, about 8-10 minutes. Drain any excess fat.

Step 2: Prepare the Buns:

While the meat is simmering, toast the whole wheat hamburger buns lightly if desired.

Step 2: Add the Sauce Ingredients:

Stir in the ketchup, brown sugar, Worcestershire sauce, mustard, water, and chili powder (if using). Season with salt and pepper to taste. Reduce the heat to low and simmer the mixture for about 10-15 minutes, or until thickened.

Step 3: Assemble the Sloppy Joes:

Spoon the meat mixture generously onto the bottom halves of the buns. Top with pickles or coleslaw if using. Cover with the top halves of the buns and serve immediately.

Per Serving:

- Calories: 400-450
- Protein: 25-30g
- Fat: 15-20g
- Carbohydrates: 35-40g
- Fiber: 4-5g
- Sodium: 700-800mg

NOTES

RATING

DIFFICULTY

Club Sandwich

PREP 15 MIN

COOK 10 MIN

2 SERVES

Benefits of Club Sandwich

Turkey: a lean source of protein,
Bacon: while bacon adds flavor, opting for turkey bacon can reduce fat intake

helps in muscle repair and growth.

Whole Wheat Buns: higher in fiber than traditional white buns

aids digestion.

Tomatoes: rich in vitamin C, potassium, and lycopene, an antioxidant.

Promote heart health.

Lettuce provides fiber and **Avocado** is high in fats

to stay fit and healthy.

Ingredients & Tools

- 6 slices of whole wheat bread, toasted
- 6 slices of cooked turkey breast (preferably low sodium)
- 6 slices of cooked bacon (opt for turkey bacon for a healthier alternative)
- 2 tomatoes, sliced
- 4 lettuce leaves (Romaine or iceberg)
- 2 tablespoons mayonnaise (or use a light or avocado-based mayo)
- Optional: slices of avocado or cucumber for extra freshness and nutrients

Tips for Success

Balanced Layers: Ensure each layer is evenly distributed to keep the sandwich stable and to distribute flavors evenly.

Healthy Substitutions: Substitute regular mayonnaise with a lighter version or use mustard for a lower-fat option.

Secure the Sandwich: Use toothpicks to help hold the sandwich together, especially if extra ingredients like avocado or cucumber are added.

It is recommended to be mindful of the sodium content, especially from the bacon and turkey. Choosing low-sodium options can help manage this. Limit your daily bread consumption to ensure you're not overloading on simple carbohydrates.

METHOD

Step 1:
Prepare the Ingredients:
Cook the bacon until crispy. Drain on paper towels to remove excess fat.
Toast the whole wheat bread until golden and crispy for better texture and flavor.

Step 2: Assemble the Sandwich:
Spread mayonnaise on three slices of toasted bread for each sandwich. On the first slice of bread, layer lettuce, two slices of turkey, and a couple of tomato slices. Top with the second slice of bread, mayonnaise side up.

Step 3: Add another layer of lettuce, bacon, and more tomato (add avocado or cucumber if using). Top with the third slice of bread, mayonnaise side down.

Step 4: Secure the sandwich with toothpicks in each quarter and carefully slice the sandwich into four triangles.
Serve immediately, ideally with a side of mixed greens or fresh fruit to balance out the meal.

Per Serving:

- Calories: 500-550
- Protein: 25-30g
- Fat: 20-25g
- Carbohydrates: 50-55g
- Fiber: 5-6g
- Sodium: 900-1000mg

NOTES

RATING

DIFFICULTY

Personal Pan Pizza

PREP 20 MIN (plus 1 hour for dough to rise)

COOK 20 MIN

1 SERVES

Benefits of Pan Pizza

Olive Oil: A healthier fat option

promotes heart health.

Whole Wheat Flour: Higher in fiber than white flour

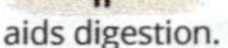

aids digestion.

Lean Proteins: Options like cooked chicken or turkey pepperoni provide protein without the high fat content of traditional meats.

For strong bones and teeth.

Vegetables: Adding a variety of vegetables increases the intake of vitamins, minerals, and fiber

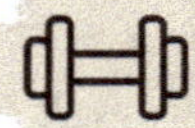

to stay fit and healthy.

Ingredients & Tools

For the Dough:

- 1 cup all-purpose flour (or use whole wheat flour for a healthier option)
- 1 teaspoon instant yeast
- 1/2 teaspoon salt
- 1/2 teaspoon sugar
- 1/2 cup warm water
- 1 tablespoon olive oil

For the Toppings:

- 1/4 cup pizza sauce (homemade or store-bought, low sodium)
- 1/2 cup shredded mozzarella cheese (reduced-fat for a healthier option)
- Toppings of choice: sliced bell peppers, onions, mushrooms, olives, cooked chicken, turkey pepperoni, spinach, etc.

Tips for Success

Dough Consistency: If the dough is too sticky, add a little more flour; if it's too dry, add a few drops of water.

Baking Surface: For the crispiest crust, use a preheated pizza stone or a cast iron skillet.

Variety of Toppings: Encourage creativity by setting up a "topping bar" so everyone can customize their own pizza.

It is recommended to be aware of portion sizes, especially with cheese and high-calorie toppings, to keep the meal balanced and healthy.

METHOD

Step 1: Prepare the Dough:
In a large bowl, combine flour, yeast, salt, and sugar. Mix well.
Add warm water and olive oil. Stir until a dough forms.
Transfer the dough to a floured surface and knead for about 5 minutes until smooth.

Step 2: Place the dough in a greased bowl, cover with a damp cloth, and let it rise in a warm place for about 1 hour or until doubled in size. Preheat your oven to 475°F (245°C).

Step 3: While the dough is rising, prepare your toppings. Once the dough has risen, punch it down and stretch or roll it out into a small circle that fits your personal pan or baking sheet.

Step 4: Spread pizza sauce over the surface of the dough, leaving a small border around the edges.
Sprinkle with cheese and arrange your toppings evenly. Bake in the preheated oven for 15-20 minutes, or until the crust is golden and the cheese is bubbly. Remove the pizza from the oven, let it cool for a few minutes, then cut into slices and serve.

Per Serving:

- Calories: 400-500
- Protein: 15-20g
- Fat: 15-20g
- Carbohydrates: 50-60g
- Fiber: 4-5g
- Sodium: 500-600mg

NOTES

RATING

DIFFICULTY

Nachos

PREP 15 MIN

COOK 10 MIN

4 SERVES

Benefits of Nachos

Avocado/Guacamole: Rich in healthy monounsaturated fats and fiber, beneficial for heart health.

Promotes heart health.

Whole Grain Chips: Provides more fiber and nutrients than regular tortilla chips.

Aids digestion.

Black Beans: High in fiber and protein.

For strong bones and teeth.

Vegetables: Adding a variety of vegetables like tomatoes, onions, and jalapeños increases intake of vitamins, minerals, and antioxidants.

to support immune system.

Ingredients & Tools

- 1 bag (about 8-10 ounces) of tortilla chips (opt for whole grain or low-sodium varieties)
- 1 cup cheddar cheese, shredded (use reduced-fat cheese for a healthier option)
- 1/2 cup black beans, rinsed and drained
- 1/2 cup corn kernels (fresh or frozen and thawed)
- 1/2 red onion, diced
- 1 jalapeño, sliced (optional)
- 1/2 cup cherry tomatoes, halved
- 1/4 cup black olives, sliced
- 1/4 cup cilantro, chopped
- 1 avocado, diced or guacamole
- Sour cream or Greek yogurt for serving (use Greek yogurt for a healthier alternative)
- Salsa for serving

Tips for Success

Layering: Properly layering the ingredients ensures every chip has a good mix of toppings.

Cheese Choice: Opt for a good melting cheese like cheddar or a mix of cheddar and Monterey Jack.

Baking Time: Keep an eye on the oven to prevent the chips from getting too brown or the cheese from burning.

It is recommended to enjoy nachos in moderation as part of a balanced diet. Nachos can be high in calories and sodium, especially if adding extra cheese and salty toppings.

METHOD

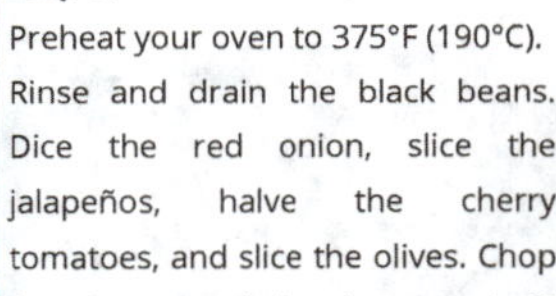

Step 1:
Preheat your oven to 375°F (190°C). Rinse and drain the black beans. Dice the red onion, slice the jalapeños, halve the cherry tomatoes, and slice the olives. Chop the cilantro and dice the avocado (if using fresh avocado).

Step 2: Spread the tortilla chips evenly on a large baking sheet.Evenly distribute the black beans, corn, and half of the diced red onion over the chips.Sprinkle the shredded cheese over the top.
Add the jalapeños and olives if using.

Step 3: Bake the Nachos:
Place the baking sheet in the oven and bake for 8-10 minutes, or until the cheese is melted and bubbly.

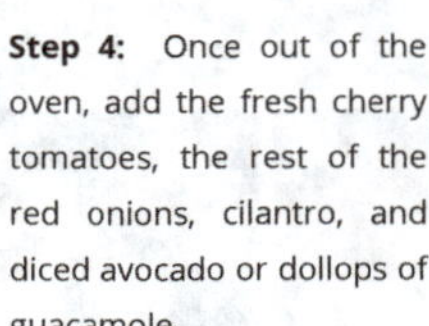

Step 4: Once out of the oven, add the fresh cherry tomatoes, the rest of the red onions, cilantro, and diced avocado or dollops of guacamole.
Serve immediately with sides of salsa and sour cream or Greek yogurt.

Per Serving:

- Calories: 300-400
- Protein: 8-12g
- Fat: 15-20g
- Carbohydrates: 30-40g
- Fiber: 4-6g
- Sodium: 400-500mg

NOTES

RATING

DIFFICULTY

Fish Tacos

PREP 20 MIN

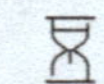
COOK 10 MIN

4 SERVES (2 TACOS EACH)

Benefits of Fish Tacos

White Fish: A lean source of protein that is low in fat and calories but high in essential nutrients like omega-3 fatty acids.

Promotes heart health.

To stay smart.

Corn Tortillas: Gluten-free and contain fiber, vitamins, and minerals.

Aids digestion.

Cabbage: Adds fiber and is rich in vitamins C and K, which help with immunity and blood clotting.

Avocado: A great source of healthy fats, fiber, and vitamins E, K, C, and B-6.

To stay strong and healthy.

Ingredients & Tools

For the Fish:

- 1 lb white fish fillets (such as tilapia, cod, or mahi-mahi)
- 1 teaspoon chili powder
- 1 teaspoon cumin
- 1/2 teaspoon garlic powder
- 1/2 teaspoon salt
- 1 tablespoon lime juice
- 1 tablespoon olive oil

For the Tacos:

- 8 small corn tortillas
- 1 cup shredded cabbage
- 1 avocado, sliced
- 1/2 cup fresh cilantro, chopped
- 1/4 cup red onion, finely chopped

For the Sauce:

- 1/2 cup Greek yogurt (or sour cream)
- 2 tablespoons lime juice
- 1 tablespoon mayonnaise
- 1/2 teaspoon garlic powder
- Salt and pepper to taste

Tips for Success

Fish Selection: Choose fresh or frozen fish fillets; fresh will have a slightly better texture and flavor but frozen is a convenient and often more affordable option.

Spice Adjustments: Adjust the spices in the marinade according to your taste preferences and desired heat level.

It is recommended to pair these tacos with a side of black beans or a fresh salsa to round out the meal. Delicious and nutritious Fish Tacos is a meal that's perfect for a healthy, satisfying lunch !

METHOD

Step 1: Marinate the Fish:

In a small bowl, combine chili powder, cumin, garlic powder, salt, and lime juice to make a marinade. Brush the fish fillets with olive oil and then rub the marinade over them. Let sit for 15-20 minutes.

Step 2: Prepare the Sauce:

In another bowl, mix together Greek yogurt, lime juice, mayonnaise, garlic powder, salt, and pepper. Set aside.

Step 3: Cook the Fish:

Heat a non-stick skillet over medium heat. Cook the marinated fish for about 4-5 minutes on each side or until it flakes easily with a fork. Remove from heat and break into smaller pieces.

Step 4: Warm the tortillas in a dry skillet or in the microwave wrapped in a damp cloth to keep them soft. Assemble the Tacos: place some fish on each tortilla, top with shredded cabbage, sliced avocado, chopped cilantro, and red onion. Drizzle with the prepared sauce.

Per Serving:

- Calories: 350-400
- Protein: 25-30g
- Fat: 15-20g
- Carbohydrates: 35-40g
- Fiber: 5-6g
- Sodium: 300-400mg

NOTES

RATING

DIFFICULTY

Submarine Sandwich

PREP 10 MIN | COOK 10 MIN | 1 SERVE

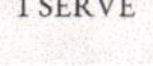

Benefits of Submarine Sandwich

Vegetables: Adding lettuce, tomatoes, and onions increases the intake of vitamins, minerals, and fiber.

To stay strong and healthy.

Cheese: Offers calcium and protein, but choose lower-fat options

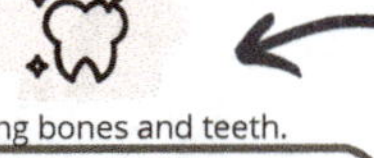

for strong bones and teeth.

Whole Wheat Bread: Provides more fiber than white bread

Aids digestion.

Turkey and Ham: Lean sources of protein

helps in muscle repair and growth.

Ingredients & Tools

- 1 large baguette or submarine roll (whole wheat for a healthier option)
- 4 slices of deli turkey breast
- 4 slices of deli ham
- 2 slices of Swiss cheese (or provolone)
- 4 slices of tomato
- 1/4 cup shredded lettuce
- Thinly sliced red onions
- 2 tablespoons mayonnaise (or use mustard or a low-fat alternative)
- 1 tablespoon Italian dressing (optional)

Tips for Success

Ingredient Variations: Feel free to customize the sandwich with different meats, cheeses, or additional vegetables like bell peppers or cucumbers.

Condiment Choices: Opt for healthier condiments like mustard or hummus to reduce fat content without sacrificing flavor.

Toasting Option: If you prefer a warm sandwich, toast the assembled sandwich in a preheated oven at 350°F (175°C) for about 5-10 minutes or until the cheese is melted.

It is recommended that you limit your daily bread consumption to ensure you're not overloading on simple carbohydrates. Pair the submarine sandwich with a side salad or vegetable sticks to balance out the meal with more fiber and nutrients.

METHOD

Step 1: Prepare the Ingredients:
Slice the baguette or submarine roll lengthwise, being careful not to cut all the way through. You want it to hinge open like a book.
Wash and slice the tomatoes and onions, and shred the lettuce.

Step 2: Assemble the Sandwich:
Spread mayonnaise (or your chosen spread) on both sides of the bread.
Layer the turkey, ham, and cheese slices on the bottom half of the bread.

Step 3: Add the tomato slices, shredded lettuce, and sliced onions.
Drizzle with Italian dressing if desired for extra flavor.

Step 4: Serve:
Close the sandwich and cut it into halves or quarters, depending on preference or if sharing.
Serve immediately, or wrap tightly in parchment paper or foil for an on-the-go meal.

Per Serving:

- Calories: 500-600
- Protein: 25-30g
- Fat: 20-25g
- Carbohydrates: 50-60g
- Fiber: 5-6g
- Sodium: 1000-1100mg

NOTES

RATING

DIFFICULTY

Gyro

PREP 20 MIN (Marinating Time: 1 hour)

COOK 10 MIN

4 SERVES

Benefits of Gyro

Olive Oil: High in monounsaturated fats

Promotes heart health

Cucumber: Provides hydration due to its high water content and is low in calories.

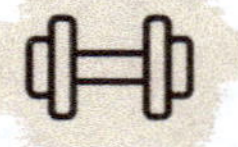

to stay fit and healthy

Greek Yogurt: Offers probiotics and is a good source of calcium.

Aids digestion

For strong bones and teeth

Protein-Rich Meat: Lamb, beef, and chicken are excellent sources of high-quality protein

helps in muscle repair and growth.

Ingredients & Tools

For the Meat:

- 1 lb lamb, beef, or chicken, thinly sliced
- 2 cloves garlic, minced
- 1 teaspoon dried oregano
- 1 teaspoon ground cumin
- 1 teaspoon paprika
- Salt and pepper to taste
- 2 tablespoons olive oil

For the Tzatziki Sauce:

- 1 cup Greek yogurt
- 1 cucumber, grated and excess water squeezed out
- 2 cloves garlic, minced
- 1 tablespoon lemon juice
- 1 tablespoon fresh dill, chopped (or 1 teaspoon dried)
- Salt and pepper to taste
- **For Serving:**
  - 4 pita bread rounds
  - 1 tomato, sliced
  - 1 small red onion, thinly sliced

Tips for Success

- **Meat Preparation:** Freezing the meat slightly can make it easier to slice thinly.
- **Alternate Cooking Method:** If you don't have a grill, cook the meat in a skillet over high heat to achieve a similar effect.

It is recommended to limit your daily bread consumption to ensure you're not overloading on simple carbohydrates. Pair the gyro with a side salad like a Greek salad to incorporate more vegetables and complete the meal with a variety of nutrients.

METHOD

Step 1: Marinate the Meat:

In a bowl, combine garlic, oregano, cumin, paprika, salt, pepper, and olive oil to make the marinade.

Add the thinly sliced meat to the marinade, ensuring it is well-coated. Cover and refrigerate for at least 1 hour, or overnight for more flavor.

Step 2: Make the Tzatziki Sauce:

In a separate bowl, mix the Greek yogurt, grated cucumber, garlic, lemon juice, and dill. Season with salt and pepper.

Refrigerate the sauce until ready to use to let the flavors meld.

Step 3: Cook the Meat:

Heat a grill pan or skillet over medium-high heat.

Remove the meat from the marinade, shaking off excess, and grill for about 2-3 minutes per side, or until fully cooked and slightly charred.

Step 4: Briefly warm the pita bread in the oven or on a skillet to make it pliable. Assemble the Gyros: Lay out the warm pita breads and spread a layer of tzatziki sauce on each. Add the cooked meat, followed by slices of tomato and onion. Roll up the pita around the fillings or fold it like a taco.

Per Serving:

- Calories: 500-600
- Protein: 30-35g
- Fat: 20-25g
- Carbohydrates: 40-45g
- Fiber: 3-4g
- Sodium: 600-700mg

NOTES

RATING

DIFFICULTY

Caprese Sandwich

PREP 10 MIN

COOK 0 MIN

2 SERVES

Benefits of Caprese Sandwich

Tomatoes: Provide vitamin C, potassium, folate, and vitamin K, along with lycopene

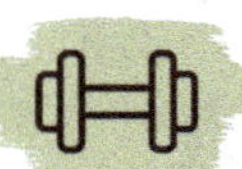

to stay fit and healthy.

Olive Oil: A source of monounsaturated fats

Promotes heart health.

Fresh Mozzarella: Offers calcium as well as protein.

For strong bones and teeth.

helps in muscle repair and growth.

Basil: Contains essential oils

anti-inflammatory and antibacterial.

Ingredients & Tools

For the Sandwich:

- 2 large ciabatta rolls (or any crusty bread like a baguette)
- 2 large tomatoes, sliced
- 8 ounces fresh mozzarella cheese, sliced
- Fresh basil leaves
- Salt and pepper to taste
- Olive oil for drizzling
- Balsamic reduction or glaze for drizzling

Tips for Success

Balsamic Reduction: If you don't have a balsamic reduction, you can easily make it by simmering balsamic vinegar over low heat until it thickens and reduces to about half its original volume.

Quality Ingredients: The simplicity of a Caprese sandwich means the quality of each ingredient shines through. Use the best quality tomatoes, mozzarella, and olive oil you can find.

It is recommended to limit your daily bread consumption to ensure you're not overloading on simple carbohydrates. Pair the sandwich with a side salad or a cup of vegetable soup to round out the meal with additional nutrients and fiber. For a lower-calorie version, use part-skim mozzarella and a lighter bread option, such as a whole-grain roll.

METHOD

Step 1: Slice the ciabatta rolls in half horizontally. If desired, lightly toast the halves to add a bit of crunch and warmth. Slice the tomatoes and mozzarella into even rounds. Wash and dry the basil leaves.

Step 2: Drizzle a little olive oil on the inside of each ciabatta half.

On the bottom halves, layer the sliced tomatoes, seasoning each layer lightly with salt and pepper. Add a layer of fresh mozzarella slices on top of the tomatoes.

Step 3: Place several basil leaves over the mozzarella.

Drizzle balsamic reduction or glaze over the basil.

Cap with the top halves of the ciabatta rolls.

Step 4: Serve:

The sandwiches can be served immediately or wrapped tightly and refrigerated for a few hours to allow the flavors to meld.

Per Serving:

- Calories: 450-500
- Protein: 20-25g
- Fat: 25-30g
- Carbohydrates: 35-40g
- Fiber: 2-3g
- Sodium: 400-500mg

NOTES

RATING

DIFFICULTY

Dinner
Chicken Parmesan

PREP 20 MIN

COOK 30 MIN

4 SERVES

Benefits of Chicken Parmesan

Chicken Breast: Provides high-quality protein

to grow and repair muscles.

Whole Wheat Ingredients: Using whole wheat flour and breadcrumbs increases fiber content

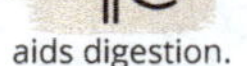

aids digestion.

Marinara Sauce: Good source of vitamin C and lycopene, especially when made with fresh tomatoes

to support immune system.

Promotes heart health.

Ingredients & Tools

For the Chicken:

- 4 boneless, skinless chicken breasts
- Salt and pepper to taste
- 1/2 cup all-purpose flour (substitute with whole wheat flour for a healthier option)
- 2 large eggs, beaten
- 1 cup breadcrumbs (use whole wheat breadcrumbs for more fiber)
- 1/2 cup grated Parmesan cheese
- 1 teaspoon dried Italian herbs
- Olive oil for frying

For Assembly:

- 2 cups marinara sauce (homemade or low-sodium store-bought)
- 1 cup shredded mozzarella cheese (use part-skim mozzarella for less fat)
- Fresh basil leaves for garnish

Tips for Success

Cheese: Adding Parmesan to the breadcrumb mix not only enhances flavor but also helps achieve a crispier crust.

Baking Instead of Frying: For a healthier version, skip frying and bake the breaded chicken in the oven at 375°F until golden and cooked through, about 20-25 minutes, then add sauce and cheese and bake until melted.

It is recommended to consider portion sizes when serving. Chicken Parmesan can be high in calories and sodium, especially with cheese and marinara sauce.

METHOD

Step 1: Flatten the chicken breasts to even thickness with a meat mallet or the with a small frying pan. Season both sides with salt and pepper. Set up three shallow dishes: one for flour, one for beaten eggs, and one for a mixture of breadcrumbs, Parmesan cheese, and Italian herbs.

Step 2: Dredge each chicken breast in flour, dip in beaten eggs, and then coat with the breadcrumb mixture.

Step 3: Cook the Chicken:
Heat a generous amount of olive oil in a large skillet over medium heat. Fry the breaded chicken breasts until golden brown on both sides and cooked through, about 4-5 minutes per side. Remove and drain on paper towels.

Step 4: Preheat your oven to 375°F (190°C). Spoon a thin layer of marinara sauce into a baking dish. Place the fried chicken breasts in the dish. Cover each breast with more marinara sauce and sprinkle with mozzarella cheese. Bake in the preheated oven for 20 minutes, or until the cheese is bubbly and slightly golden. Serve hot.

Per Serving:

- Calories: 450-500
- Protein: 35-40g
- Fat: 20-25g
- Carbohydrates: 30-35g
- Fiber: 3-4g
- Sodium: 700-800mg

NOTES

RATING

DIFFICULTY

Classic Pizza

PREP 1 H 30 MIN

COOK 20 MIN

8 SERVES

Benefits of Classic Pizza

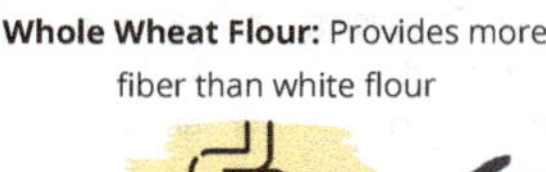

Whole Wheat Flour: Provides more fiber than white flour

Aids digestion.

Olive Oil: A source of monounsaturated fats

Promotes heart health.

Tomatoes: Provide vitamin C, potassium, folate, and vitamin K, along with lycopene

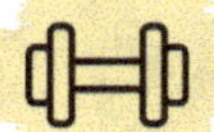

to stay fit and healthy.

Vegetables: Adding vegetables like bell peppers and mushrooms increases the intake of vitamins, minerals, and fiber.

to support immune system.

Ingredients & Tools

For the Dough:

- 2 1/4 cups whole wheat flour
- 1 packet (2 1/4 teaspoons) active dry yeast
- 1 teaspoon sugar
- 3/4 teaspoon salt
- 1 cup warm water
- 2 tablespoons olive oil

For the Sauce:

- 1 can (15 oz) crushed tomatoes
- 1 teaspoon dried oregano
- 1 teaspoon dried basil
- 1 clove garlic, minced
- Salt and pepper to taste

Toppings:

- 1 1/2 cups shredded mozzarella cheese
- 1/2 cup sliced bell peppers
- 1/2 cup sliced mushrooms
- 1/2 cup sliced black olives
- Additional options: onions, pepperoni, cooked sausage, fresh basil

Tips for Success

Dough Thickness: For a crispier crust, roll the dough thinner. For a thicker, chewier crust, leave it a bit thicker.

Avoid Sogginess: Don't overload with sauce or toppings, as this can make the dough soggy.

It is recommended to limit your daily bread consumption to ensure you're not overloading on simple carbohydrates. Serve with a side salad to incorporate more fresh vegetables into your meal.

METHOD

Step 1: In a large bowl, combine the flour, yeast, sugar, and salt. Add warm water and olive oil, and stir until the dough begins to form. Turn out onto a floured surface and knead for about 5 minutes until smooth and elastic. Place in a greased bowl, cover, and let rise in a warm place until doubled, about 1 hour.

Step 2: Make the Sauce: Combine crushed tomatoes, oregano, basil, minced garlic, salt, and pepper in a saucepan. Simmer over low heat for 15-20 minutes while the dough rises.

Step 3: Preheat your oven to 475°F (245°C). If you have a pizza stone, place it in the oven to heat. Punch down the dough and roll it out on a floured surface to fit your pizza stone or baking sheet. Spread the sauce evenly over the dough. Sprinkle with mozzarella cheese and arrange your chosen toppings.

Step 4: Bake in the preheated oven for 12-15 minutes or until the crust is golden and cheese is bubbly and slightly browned.

Let the pizza cool for a few minutes before slicing and serving.

Per Serving:

- Calories: 250-300
- Protein: 10-12g
- Fat: 10-12g
- Carbohydrates: 30-35g
- Fiber: 2-3g
- Sodium: 400-500mg

NOTES

RATING

DIFFICULTY

Lasagna

PREP 30 MIN

COOK 45 MIN

8 SERVES

Benefits of Lasagna

Garlic and Onions: Offer anti-inflammatory properties

to support immune system.

Cheese: Good source of calcium and protein.

For strong bones and teeth.

Lean Protein: Using ground turkey or part-skim dairy products helps reduce fat intake while still providing high-quality protein

to grow and repair muscles.

Tomatoes: Provide vitamin C, potassium, folate, and vitamin K, along with lycopene

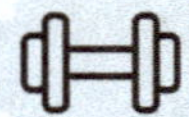

to stay fit and healthy.

Ingredients & Tools

For the Meat Sauce:

- 1 lb ground beef (or use ground turkey for a leaner option)
- 1 onion, chopped
- 2 cloves garlic, minced
- 1 can (28 oz) crushed tomatoes
- 2 tablespoons tomato paste
- 1 teaspoon dried basil
- 1 teaspoon dried oregano
- Salt and pepper to taste
- 1/2 cup red wine (optional)

For the Cheese Mixture:

- 15 oz ricotta cheese
- 1 egg
- 1/2 cup grated Parmesan cheese
- 1 tablespoon chopped fresh parsley

Additional Ingredients:

- 9-12 lasagna noodles, cooked according to package instructions
- 2 cups shredded mozzarella cheese (use part-skim for less fat)
- Fresh basil for garnish (optional)

Tips for Success

Noodle Tip: Use oven-ready lasagna noodles to skip the boiling step, making assembly quicker and cleaner.

Sauce Consistency: Ensure the meat sauce is not too watery to prevent a soggy lasagna.

It is recommended to enjoy lasagna in moderation, especially if managing dietary restrictions since it is rich in calories and sodium. Pair a slice of lasagna with a side salad or steamed vegetables to incorporate more fiber and nutrients into your meal.

METHOD

Step 1: Prepare the Meat Sauce:
In a large skillet, cook the ground beef, onion, and garlic over medium heat until the meat is browned and the onions are translucent. Drain any excess fat. Stir in the crushed tomatoes, tomato paste, basil, oregano, salt, pepper, and red wine if using. Simmer for 20 minutes until the flavors are well blended.

Step 2: Prepare the Cheese Mixture: In a bowl, mix together the ricotta cheese, egg, Parmesan cheese, and parsley. Set aside.

Preheat your oven to 375°F (190°C).

Step 3: In a 9x13 inch baking dish, spread a layer of meat sauce on the bottom. Layer cooked lasagna noodles over the sauce. Spread a layer of the ricotta cheese mixture over the noodles, then sprinkle with mozzarella cheese. Repeat the layering process until all ingredients are used, finishing with a top layer of meat sauce and mozzarella cheese.

Step 4: Cover with foil and bake in the preheated oven for 25 minutes. Remove the foil and bake for an additional 20 minutes, or until the cheese is bubbly and golden brown. Let the lasagna sit for 15 minutes before slicing. This helps the layers set and makes it easier to serve. Garnish with fresh basil if desired and serve warm.

Per Serving:

- Calories: 450-500
- Protein: 25-30g
- Fat: 20-25g
- Carbohydrates: 35-40g
- Fiber: 3-4g
- Sodium: 600-700mg

NOTES

RATING

DIFFICULTY

Oven-Baked Ribs

PREP 15 MIN

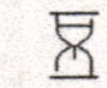
COOK 3 HOURS

12 SERVES

Benefits of Oven-Baked Ribs

Pork Ribs: Good source of high-quality protein and essential vitamins such as B6 and B12

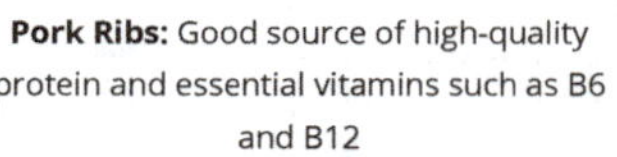

To stay smart.

To feel energized for long time.

Spices in Dry Rub: Provide antioxidants

to fight off inflammations.

Spices like paprika and cumin also add rich flavor without extra calories or sodium

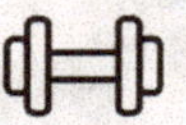

to stay fit .

Ingredients & Tools

For the Ribs:

- 2 racks of pork ribs (about 3-4 pounds each)
- Salt and pepper to taste

For the Dry Rub:

- 2 tablespoons brown sugar (or substitute with coconut sugar for a healthier option)
- 1 tablespoon paprika
- 1 teaspoon garlic powder
- 1 teaspoon onion powder
- 1 teaspoon ground cumin

For the Barbecue Sauce:

- 1 cup ketchup (look for low-sodium or organic versions)
- 2 tablespoons apple cider vinegar
- 2 tablespoons Worcestershire sauce
- 1 tablespoon honey (or maple syrup)
- 1 teaspoon smoked paprika
- Salt and pepper to taste

Tips for Success

Low and Slow: Cooking the ribs at a low temperature for a longer duration helps them become tender and flavorful.

Basting: Regular basting with barbecue sauce during the final cooking stage adds layers of flavor and helps create a deliciously sticky crust.

It is recommended to use homemade barbecue sauce. By making your own sauce, you control the ingredients and can limit the amount of sugar and sodium compared to store-bought versions.

METHOD

Step 1: Remove the membrane from the back of each rack of ribs by loosening it with a knife and pulling it off. Season both sides of the ribs with salt and pepper. In a small bowl, mix together the brown sugar, paprika, garlic powder, onion powder, ground cumin, and cayenne pepper. Rub this mixture all over both sides of the ribs, pressing it into the meat.

Step 2: Pre-Bake the Ribs:
Preheat your oven to 275°F (135°C).
Wrap each rack of ribs tightly in aluminum foil and place them on a baking sheet.
Bake in the preheated oven for about 2.5 hours, or until the meat is tender and pulls away from the bones.

Step 3: Make the Barbecue Sauce:
While the ribs are baking, combine the ketchup, apple cider vinegar, Worcestershire sauce, honey, smoked paprika, salt, and pepper in a saucepan.
Simmer over low heat for 10-15 minutes, stirring occasionally until the sauce thickens slightly.

Step 4: Remove the ribs from the oven and increase the oven temperature to 350°F (175°C). Carefully unwrap the ribs and brush them generously with the barbecue sauce. Return the ribs to the oven, uncovered, and bake for an additional 30 minutes. Let the ribs rest for a few minutes before slicing between the bones. Serve with extra barbecue sauce.

Per Serving:

- Calories: 500-600
- Protein: 40-45g
- Fat: 35-40g
- Carbohydrates: 20-25g
- Fiber: 1-2g
- Sodium: 500-600mg

NOTES

RATING

DIFFICULTY

Fajitas

PREP 20 MIN (plus marinating time) | COOK 10 MIN | 4 SERVES

Benefits of Fajitas

Lean Proteins: Chicken, beef, or shrimp provide high-quality protein

to grow and repair muscles

Bell Peppers and Onions: Rich in vitamins C and K, fiber, and antioxidants

to support immune system

Avocado is a superfood. It contains vitamins C, E, K, and B-6, as well as riboflavin, niacin, folate, pantothenic acid, magnesium, and potassium.

To have healthy skin, hair, and nails.

Olive Oil: Contains heart-healthy monounsaturated fats.

Promotes heart health

Ingredients & Tools

For the Fajitas:

- 1 lb chicken breasts, thinly sliced (can also use beef skirt steak or shrimp)
- 3 bell peppers (choose different colors for variety), sliced
- 1 large onion, sliced
- 2 tablespoons olive oil
- 1 lime, juiced
- Salt and pepper to taste

For the Marinade:

- 2 cloves garlic, minced
- 1 teaspoon chili powder
- 1 teaspoon paprika
- 1/2 teaspoon ground cumin
- 1/2 teaspoon dried oregano
- Salt and pepper to taste
- 2 tablespoons olive oil
- Juice of 1 lime

For Serving:

- Flour tortillas (use whole wheat tortillas for a healthier option)
- Optional toppings: avocado slices, salsa, sour cream, cilantro, cheese

Tips for Success

Protein Variations: Mix and match proteins to keep it interesting—try combining chicken and shrimp for a varied flavor profile.

Marinating Time: Don't skip the marinating as it adds flavor and tenderness to the meat.

High Heat Cooking: Cook the vegetables on high heat for a quick char without overcooking them, maintaining their crunch and nutrients.

To keep calories in check, consider the size of the tortillas and the overall portion. Use whole wheat tortillas to reduce calories.

METHOD

Step 1: Marinate the Meat:

In a bowl, combine all the marinade ingredients. Add the sliced chicken (or other protein) and toss to coat evenly. Cover and refrigerate for at least 1 hour, or up to 4 hours.

Prepare the Vegetables:

Slice the bell peppers and onion.

Step 2: Cook the Chicken:

Heat 1 tablespoon olive oil in a large skillet over medium-high heat. Remove the chicken from the marinade (discard the marinade) and cook until browned and cooked through, about 4-5 minutes per side. Remove from the skillet and set aside.

Step 3:

In the same skillet, add the remaining olive oil, sliced bell peppers, and onion. Sauté until vegetables are tender and slightly charred, about 5-7 minutes. Return the chicken to the skillet, add lime juice, and stir to combine. Cook for an additional 2 minutes.

Step 4:

Warm the tortillas in a dry skillet or microwave, wrapped in a damp cloth to keep them soft. Spoon the chicken and vegetable mixture onto each tortilla. Top with your choice of avocado, salsa, sour cream, cilantro, or cheese. Serve the fajitas immediately with lime wedges on the side for extra flavor.

Per Serving:

- Calories: 350-400
- Protein: 30-35g
- Fat: 15-20g
- Carbohydrates: 25-30g
- Fiber: 4-5g
- Sodium: 400-500mg

NOTES

RATING

DIFFICULTY

Beef Stroganoff

PREP 20 MIN

COOK 20 MIN

4 SERVES

Benefits of Beef Stroganoff

Lean Beef: Provides high-quality protein and is a good source of iron

to grow and repair muscles.

To feel energized.

Mushrooms: Offer a good source of B vitamins, selenium, potassium, and antioxidants.

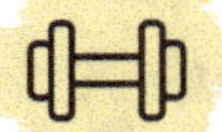

to stay fit and healthy.

Whole Wheat Flour and Noodles: Higher in fiber than their refined counterparts

Aid digestion.

Ingredients & Tools

For the Beef Stroganoff:

- 1 lb beef sirloin, thinly sliced
- 2 tablespoons olive oil
- 1 medium onion, finely chopped
- 2 cups mushrooms, sliced
- 1 clove garlic, minced
- 1 tablespoon all-purpose flour (substitute with whole wheat flour for a healthier option)
- 1 cup beef broth (low sodium)
- 1 tablespoon Worcestershire sauce
- 1 teaspoon Dijon mustard
- 1/2 cup sour cream (use light sour cream to reduce fat)
- Salt and pepper to taste
- Fresh parsley, chopped (for garnish)

For Serving:

- Egg noodles, cooked (use whole wheat noodles for a healthier option) Alternatively, serve with brown rice or mashed potatoes

Tips for Success

Slicing the Beef: Freeze the beef for 20-30 minutes before slicing; it makes it easier to cut thin, even slices.

Sour Cream: Add the sour cream off the heat to prevent it from curdling.

Thickening the Sauce: If the sauce is too thin after simmering, you can let it reduce further or adjust the thickness with a little more flour mixed with water.

It is recommended to be mindful of portion sizes, especially with the noodles or rice, to keep calories in check. Complement the dish with a side of steamed green vegetables like green beans or broccoli to add color and nutrients.

METHOD

Step 1: Prepare the Beef:

Season the beef slices with salt and pepper.

Heat 1 tablespoon olive oil in a large skillet over medium-high heat. Add the beef and sear until browned. Remove the beef from the skillet and set aside.

Step 2: Cook the Vegetables:

In the same skillet, add the remaining olive oil, chopped onion, and sliced mushrooms. Sauté until the onions are translucent and mushrooms are browned, about 5-7 minutes.

Add the minced garlic and cook for another minute until fragrant.

Step 3:

Sprinkle the flour over the vegetables and stir to coat. Cook for 1-2 minutes. Slowly add the beef broth, stirring continuously. Bring to a simmer. Stir in the Worcestershire sauce and Dijon mustard. Reduce heat and let simmer gently for 5 minutes.

Step 4:

Return the beef to the skillet and warm through. Remove from heat and stir in the sour cream. Adjust seasoning with salt and pepper. Garnish with chopped fresh parsley. Serve the beef stroganoff over cooked egg noodles, brown rice, or mashed potatoes.

Per Serving:

- Calories: 400-450
- Protein: 25-30g
- Fat: 20-25g
- Carbohydrates: 20-30g
- Fiber: 2-3g
- Sodium: 300-400mg

NOTES

RATING

DIFFICULTY

Shrimp Scampi

PREP 15 MIN | COOK 15 MIN | 4 SERVES

Shrimp: Provides high-quality protein and is low in calories. Shrimp is also a good source of omega-3 fatty acids

To grow and repair muscles.

To stay smart.

Olive Oil: Contains monounsaturated fats that can help reduce bad cholesterol levels

Promotes heart health.

Lemon being high in vitamin C and **Garlic** known for its health benefits.

Protect immune system.

Ingredients & Tools

For the Shrimp Scampi:

- 1 lb large shrimp, peeled and deveined
- Salt and pepper to taste
- 3 tablespoons olive oil
- 4 cloves garlic, minced
- 1/2 cup low-sodium chicken broth (or white wine)
- Juice and zest of 1 lemon
- 3 tablespoons unsalted butter (use less or substitute with olive oil
- 1/4 cup chopped fresh parsley
- Red pepper flakes to taste (optional for a bit of heat)
- For Serving:
- 8 oz spaghetti or angel hair pasta (use whole wheat pasta for a healthier option)
- Freshly grated Parmesan cheese (optional)
- Additional lemon wedges for serving

Tips for Success

Shrimp Cooking Time: Be careful not to overcook the shrimp, as they can become tough. They cook quickly and are done as soon as they turn pink.

Sauce Consistency: Adjust the thickness of the sauce by adding more or less pasta water until you achieve the desired consistency.

It is recommended to be mindful of the total fat content, especially from butter and oil, to keep the meal balanced. Pair this dish with a side of steamed vegetables or a fresh salad to increase fiber and nutrient intake.

METHOD

Step 1: Prepare the Pasta:
Cook the pasta according to package instructions until al dente. Drain, reserving a little pasta water, and set aside.

Step 2: Cook the Shrimp:
Season the shrimp with salt and pepper. Heat olive oil in a large skillet over medium-high heat. Add the shrimp and cook until they are pink and opaque, about 2 minutes per side. Remove the shrimp from the skillet and set aside.

Step 3: In the same skillet, add the minced garlic and red pepper flakes if using. Sauté for about 1 minute. Pour in the chicken broth or white wine, and add the lemon juice. Let the sauce simmer for about 3 minutes or until slightly reduced. Stir in the butter until melted. Return the shrimp to the skillet, add the chopped parsley and lemon zest, and toss to coat.

Step 4: Add the cooked pasta to the skillet with the shrimp and sauce. Toss well to combine. If the dish seems dry, add a little reserved pasta water to help the sauce cling to the pasta. Serve immediately, garnished with freshly grated Parmesan cheese and additional parsley if desired. Offer lemon wedges on the side for extra zing.

Per Serving:

- Calories: 450-500
- Protein: 25-30g
- Fat: 20-25g
- Carbohydrates: 40-45g
- Fiber: 2-3g
- Sodium: 300-400mg

NOTES

RATING

DIFFICULTY

Fried Chicken

PREP 15 MIN

COOK 30 MIN

4 SERVES

Benefits of Fried Chicken

Chicken: A good source of high-quality protein

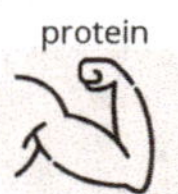

To grow and repair muscles .

Buttermilk is good source of calcium

For strong bones and teeth.

Whole Grains: Using whole wheat or corn tortillas adds fiber

Aids digestion.

For prolonged satiety .

Ingredients & Tools

For the Chicken:

- 8 pieces of chicken (mix of thighs, drumsticks, and breasts)
- 2 cups buttermilk
- 1 tablespoon salt
- 1 tablespoon black pepper
- 1 tablespoon paprika
- 1 teaspoon garlic powder

For the Coating:

- 2 cups all-purpose flour (use whole wheat flour for a healthier option)
- 1 teaspoon salt
- 1 teaspoon black pepper
- 1 teaspoon paprika
- 1/2 teaspoon cayenne pepper (optional for heat)
- Oil for frying (vegetable or canola oil)

Tips for Success

Marinating Time: The longer the chicken marinates, the more tender and flavorful it will be.

Oil Temperature: Maintain a steady temperature while frying to ensure the chicken cooks evenly and doesn't absorb excess oil.

It is recommended to enjoy fried chicken in moderation as part of a balanced diet due to its high calorie and fat content. Serve with a side of steamed vegetables or a fresh salad to balance out the richness of the fried chicken.

METHOD

Step 1: Marinate the Chicken:

In a large bowl, mix buttermilk with salt, pepper, paprika, and garlic powder.

Add the chicken pieces, ensuring they are fully submerged. Cover and refrigerate for at least 4 hours, preferably overnight.

Step 2: Prepare the Coating:

In a separate large bowl, combine the flour, salt, pepper, paprika, and cayenne pepper.

Take each piece of chicken out of the buttermilk, letting excess drip off.

Dredge thoroughly in the flour mixture, then shake off the excess.

Step 3: Fry the Chicken:

Heat oil in a deep fryer or large pot to 350°F (175°C).

Working in batches, carefully place the chicken pieces in the hot oil. Fry until golden brown and cooked through, about 15-18 minutes for larger pieces and 8-10 minutes for smaller pieces. The internal temperature should reach 165°F (74°C).

Step 4: Remove the chicken from the oil and drain on paper towels to remove excess oil.

Serve hot, garnished with slices of lemon or a sprinkle of fresh parsley if desired.

Per Serving:

- Calories: 500-600
- Protein: 25-35g
- Fat: 30-40g
- Carbohydrates: 30-40g
- Fiber: 1-2g
- Sodium: 800-900mg

NOTES

RATING

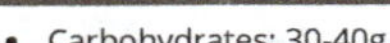

DIFFICULTY

Spaghetti and Meatballs

PREP 30 MIN

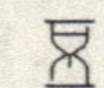
COOK 60 MIN

4 SERVES

Benefits of Spaghetti and Meatballs

Lean Ground Beef/Turkey: Provides high-quality protein

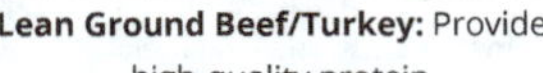

To grow and repair muscles.

Provides a longer feeling of satiety.

Tomatoes: Provide vitamin C, potassium, folate, and vitamin K, along with lycopene

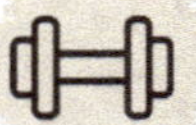

to stay fit and healthy.

Whole wheat: Using whole wheat spaghetti adds fiber

Aids digestion.

Ingredients & Tools

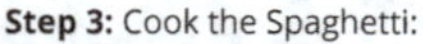

For the Meatballs:

- 1 lb ground beef (or mix of beef and pork for flavor, or ground turkey)
- 1/2 cup whole wheat breadcrumbs
- 1/4 cup grated Parmesan cheese
- 1 large egg
- 2 cloves garlic, minced
- 1/4 cup fresh parsley, chopped
- Salt and pepper to taste

For the Sauce:

- 2 tablespoons olive oil
- 1 onion, finely chopped
- 2 cloves garlic, minced
- 1 can (28 ounces) crushed tomatoes
- 1 teaspoon dried basil
- 1 teaspoon dried oregano
- Salt and pepper to taste

For Serving:

- 12 oz spaghetti (use whole wheat spaghetti for more nutrients)
- Fresh basil or parsley for garnish
- Additional grated Parmesan cheese

Tips for Success

Searing Meatballs: Searing the meatballs before adding to the sauce helps to develop flavor and texture.

Simmering Sauce: Letting the sauce simmer with the meatballs enhances the depth of flavor, making the meatballs tender and savory.

It is recommended to enjoy it in moderation, especially if watching your caloric intake, as the dish is calorie-dense. Serve with a side salad or steamed vegetables to add more fiber and vitamins to your meal.

METHOD

Step 1: Make the Meatballs:

In a large bowl, combine ground meat, breadcrumbs, Parmesan, egg, minced garlic, chopped parsley, salt, and pepper. Mix well until evenly combined. Form into 1.5-inch balls.

In a skillet, heat some olive oil over medium heat. Add meatballs and brown on all sides. Remove and set aside.

Step 2: Prepare the Sauce:

In the same skillet, add more olive oil if needed. Sauté onion and garlic until translucent. Add crushed tomatoes, basil, oregano, salt, and pepper. Bring to a simmer. Return meatballs to the skillet, cover, and simmer for 30-40 minutes until meatballs are cooked through.

Step 3: Cook the Spaghetti:

While the sauce simmers, bring a large pot of salted water to a boil. Cook spaghetti according to package instructions until al dente.

Drain and set aside.

Step 4:

Place cooked spaghetti on plates. Top with meatballs and sauce. Garnish with fresh basil or parsley and sprinkle with additional Parmesan cheese.

Per Serving:

- Calories: 600-650
- Protein: 35-40g
- Fat: 25-30g
- Carbohydrates: 65-70g
- Fiber: 6-7g
- Sodium: 800-900mg

NOTES

RATING

DIFFICULTY

Chicken Tacos

PREP 20 MIN

COOK 15 MIN

4 SERVES

Benefits of Chicken Tacos

Whole Wheat Tortillas: Offers more fiber and nutrients than corn tortillas.

Aids digestion

Avocado is a superfood. It contains vitamins C, E, K, and B-6, as well as riboflavin, niacin, folate, pantothenic acid, magnesium, and potassium.

To have healthy skin, hair, and nails.

Dairy: Low-fat cheese and Greek yogurt provide calcium and protein without excessive saturated fat.

For strong bones and teeth.

Chicken Breast: A lean source of protein.

To grow and repair muscles.

Ingredients & Tools

For the Chicken:

- 1 lb boneless, skinless chicken breasts, thinly sliced or shredded
- 1 tablespoon olive oil
- 1 teaspoon chili powder
- 1 teaspoon cumin
- 1/2 teaspoon paprika
- 1/4 teaspoon garlic powder
- Salt and pepper to taste
- Juice of 1 lime

For Serving:

- 8-10 small corn tortillas (or whole wheat tortillas for added fiber)
- Shredded lettuce or cabbage
- Diced tomatoes
- Diced red onion
- Chopped cilantro
- Sliced avocado or guacamole
- Low-fat sour cream or Greek yogurt
- Salsa or pico de gallo
- Lime wedges for additional flavor

Tips for Success

Meat Alternatives: For a vegetarian option, substitute chicken meat with cooked lentils or a meat substitute like textured vegetable protein (TVP).

Enhance Flavors: Customize the spices according to your preference. Adding a bit of smoked paprika can give a nice depth to the flavor.

It is recommended to be mindful of portion sizes, especially with toppings like cheese and sour cream, to keep the meal balanced. Pair the tacos with a side of black beans or a fresh corn salad to round out the meal with extra fiber and protein.

METHOD

Step 1: Marinate the Chicken:
In a bowl, mix the olive oil, chili powder, cumin, paprika, garlic powder, salt, pepper, and lime juice. Add the chicken and toss to coat. Let it marinate for at least 15 minutes, or up to an hour if time allows.

Step 2: Cook the Chicken:
Heat a skillet over medium-high heat. Add the marinated chicken and cook for 5-7 minutes on each side, or until fully cooked and slightly charred. If using shredded pre-cooked chicken, just heat it through in the skillet with the marinade for added flavor.

Step 3: Prepare the Tortillas:
Warm the tortillas in a dry skillet or microwave wrapped in a damp cloth to keep them soft and pliable. Spoon the cooked chicken onto each tortilla. Top with shredded lettuce, diced tomatoes, red onion, cilantro, and avocado.

Step 4: Add a dollop of Greek yogurt and a spoonful of salsa or pico de gallo. Serve the tacos immediately with lime wedges on the side for squeezing over the top.

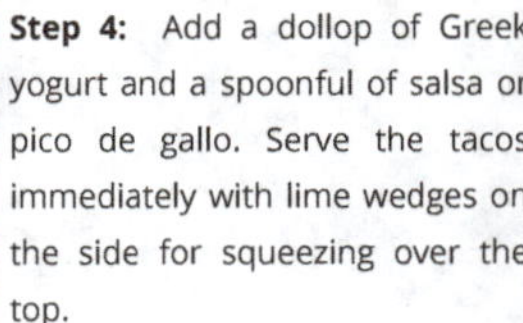

Per Serving:

- Calories: 300-350
- Protein: 25-30g
- Fat: 10-15g
- Carbohydrates: 25-30g
- Fiber: 3-4g
- Sodium: 200-300mg

NOTES

RATING

DIFFICULTY

Baked Ziti

PREP 30 MIN

COOK 30 MIN

8 SERVES

Benefits of Baked Ziti

Whole Wheat Spaghetti: Offers more fiber and nutrients than regular pasta

Aids digestion

Tomatoes: High in vitamin C, potassium, folate, and vitamin K, and a great source of antioxidants, including lycopene.

Promotes heart health

Cheese: Good source of calcium and protein; opting for part-skim options helps reduce fat intake without sacrificing flavor.

For strong bones and teeth.

Using **ground turkey** instead of beef reduces fat content, particularly saturated fat, and still provides high-quality protein.

To grow and repair muscles .

Ingredients & Tools

For the Pasta and Sauce:

- 1 lb ziti or penne pasta (use whole wheat pasta for a healthier option)
- 2 tablespoons olive oil
- 1 onion, chopped
- 2 cloves garlic, minced
- 1 lb ground beef or turkey (use turkey for a leaner option)
- 1 can (28 ounces) crushed tomatoes
- 1 teaspoon dried basil
- 1 teaspoon dried oregano
- Salt and pepper to taste

For the Cheese Layer:

- 15 oz ricotta cheese (use part-skim ricotta for less fat)
- 1 egg, beaten
- 1/2 cup grated Parmesan cheese
- 2 cups shredded mozzarella cheese (use part-skim mozzarella for less fat)
- Fresh basil or parsley, chopped (for garnish)

Tips for Success

Pasta Cook Time: Be careful not to overcook the pasta since it will cook further in the oven. Undercooking it slightly ensures it remains firm after baking.

Layering: Proper layering ensures each serving has a good mix of pasta, sauce, and cheese.

It is recommended to consider serving smaller portions if managing calorie intake, as this dish is rich and hearty. Serve with a side salad or steamed vegetables to add fiber and vitamins, creating a balanced meal.

METHOD

Step 1: Prepare the Pasta: Preheat oven to 375°F (190°C). Cook the ziti according to package instructions until just al dente. Drain and set aside.

Step 2: Prepare the sauce: In a large skillet, heat the olive oil over medium heat. Add the onion and garlic, sautéing until soft and translucent. Add the ground beef or turkey, breaking it up with a spoon. Cook until browned. Stir in the crushed tomatoes, basil, oregano, salt, and pepper. Simmer for about 10 minutes.

Step 3: In a bowl, combine the ricotta cheese, beaten egg, and Parmesan cheese. In a large baking dish, spread a thin layer of the sauce. Mix the cooked pasta with the remaining sauce and half of the shredded mozzarella. Pour this mixture into the baking dish. Spread the ricotta mixture evenly over the pasta.

Step 4: Sprinkle the remaining mozzarella cheese on top. Cover with foil and bake for 20 minutes. Remove the foil and bake for an additional 10 minutes, or until the cheese is bubbly and golden. Let the baked ziti rest for 10 minutes before serving. Garnish with chopped fresh basil or parsley.

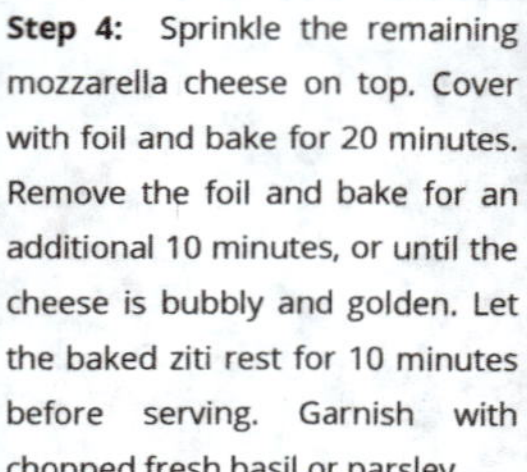

Per Serving:

- Calories: 450-500
- Protein: 25-30g
- Fat: 20-25g
- Carbohydrates: 40-45g
- Fiber: 5-6g
- Sodium: 600-700mg

NOTES

RATING

DIFFICULTY

Enchiladas

PREP 30 MIN

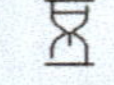
COOK 20 MIN

6 SERVES

Benefits of Enchiladas

Whole Wheat Flour: Offers more fiber and nutrients than refined flours

Aids digestion.

Black Beans and Corn: Provide fiber, protein, and essential nutrients like iron and potassium.

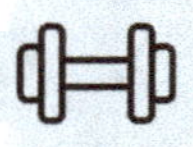

to stay fit and healthy.

Low-Fat Cheese: Reduces the calorie and fat content without sacrificing flavor.

For strong bones and teeth

Chicken Breast: A lean source of high-quality protein.

To grow and repair muscles.

Ingredients & Tools

For the Filling:

- 2 cups cooked, shredded chicken
- 1 cup black beans, rinsed and drained
- 1 cup corn kernels (fresh or frozen)
- 1/2 cup diced red onion
- 1/2 cup chopped cilantro
- 1 teaspoon cumin
- 1 teaspoon chili powder
- Salt and pepper to taste

For the Sauce:

- 2 tablespoons olive oil
- 2 tablespoons of flour (opt for whole-wheat)
- 1 can (8 ounces) tomato sauce
- 2 cups vegetable broth (low sodium)
- 2 tablespoons chili powder
- 1 teaspoon cumin
- 1/2 teaspoon garlic powder
- Salt to taste

Additional:

- 8-10 corn tortillas
- 2 cups shredded low-fat cheese
- Sour cream or Greek yogurt
- Chopped green onions, additional cilantro, or sliced avocado for garnish

Tips for Success

Softening Tortillas: Properly softening the tortillas is key to preventing them from breaking during assembly. Heating them makes them more flexible.

Sauce Thickness: Adjust the thickness of the sauce with more flour or broth, depending on your preference. The sauce should coat the back of a spoon but still be pourable.

It is recommended to consider the portion sizes, especially if monitoring caloric and sodium intake. Serve enchiladas with a side of a fresh green salad or steamed vegetables to balance out the meal.

METHOD

Step 1: Prepare the Sauce:
Heat olive oil in a saucepan over medium heat. Stir in flour and cook for 1 minute. Add tomato sauce, vegetable broth, chili powder, cumin, garlic powder, and salt. Whisk until smooth. Bring to a simmer and cook until slightly thickened, about 5-7 minutes. Remove from heat and set aside.

Step 2: Prepare the Filling:
In a bowl, combine the shredded chicken, black beans, corn, red onion, cilantro, cumin, chili powder, salt, and pepper. Mix well. Preheat the oven to 375°F (190°C). Warm the tortillas in a microwave or over an open flame to make them pliable.

Step 3: Dip each tortilla in the prepared sauce, then lay flat and place a portion of the filling and a sprinkle of cheese in the center. Roll up tightly and place seam-side down in a baking dish. Pour the remaining sauce over the enchiladas and sprinkle with the remaining cheese.

Step 4: Cover with foil and bake for 15 minutes. Remove the foil and bake for an additional 5 minutes or until the cheese is bubbly and slightly golden. Let cool slightly before serving. Garnish with sour cream or Greek yogurt, green onions, additional cilantro, or sliced avocado.

Per Serving:

- Calories: 350-400
- Protein: 25-30g
- Fat: 15-20g
- Carbohydrates: 30-35g
- Fiber: 6-7g
- Sodium: 600-700mg

NOTES

RATING

DIFFICULTY

Roast Chicken

PREP 15 MIN

COOK 1 HOUR 30 MIN

4-6 SERVES

Benefits of Roast Chicken

Olive Oil: A good source of monounsaturated fats

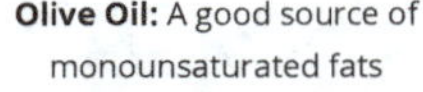

Promotes heart health

Garlic and Herbs: Offer anti-inflammatory and antioxidant benefits

To support immune system

Vegetables: Supply fiber, vitamins, and minerals that contribute to a balanced diet.

to stay fit and healthy

Chicken: Provides high-quality protein. Rich in various vitamins and minerals, including B vitamins.

To grow and repair muscles. For energy production

Ingredients & Tools

For the Chicken:

- 1 whole chicken (about 4-5 pounds)
- 2 tablespoons olive oil
- 1 lemon, halved
- 4 cloves garlic, smashed
- Fresh herbs (such as rosemary, thyme, and sage)
- Salt and pepper to taste

For the Vegetables (optional):

- 2 carrots, peeled and cut into chunks
- 2 onions, peeled and quartered
- 1 pound potatoes, peeled and halved
- Olive oil
- Salt and pepper

Tips for Success

Ensuring Moisture: To ensure the chicken remains moist, baste it periodically with the juices from the pan during roasting.

Herb Variations: Experiment with different herbs for varied flavors. Each type of herb can add a unique dimension to the roast.

It is recommended to remove the skin before eating to significantly reduce fat content. Pair the roast chicken with a side of steamed green vegetables like broccoli or green beans to enhance the meal with more nutrients.

METHOD

Step 1: Preheat your oven to 375°F (190°C). Remove the giblets from inside the chicken and pat the outside dry with paper towels. Rub the chicken all over with olive oil, then season inside and out with salt and pepper. Stuff the cavity with the lemon halves, smashed garlic, and fresh herbs.

Step 2: Prepare the Vegetables (if using):

Toss the carrots, onions, and potatoes with olive oil, salt, and pepper.

Spread them in a roasting pan, creating a bed for the chicken.

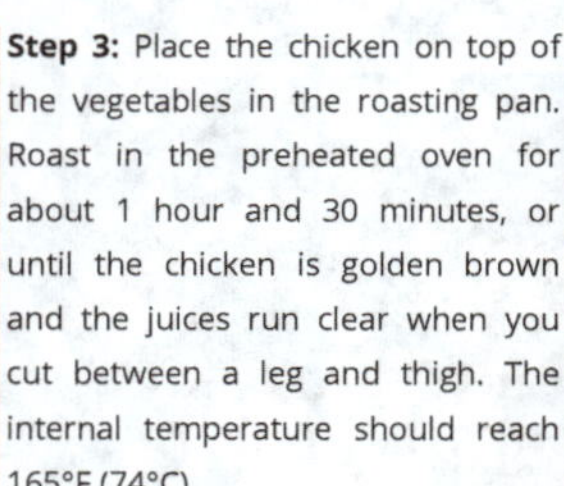

Step 3: Place the chicken on top of the vegetables in the roasting pan. Roast in the preheated oven for about 1 hour and 30 minutes, or until the chicken is golden brown and the juices run clear when you cut between a leg and thigh. The internal temperature should reach 165°F (74°C).

Step 4: Let the chicken rest for 10-15 minutes before carving. This helps the juices redistribute throughout the meat, making it more tender and flavorful. Serve with the roasted vegetables.

Per Serving:

- Calories: 300-350 (without skin)
- Protein: 25-30g
- Fat: 20-25g
- Carbohydrates: 15-20g (if including vegetables)
- Fiber: 2-3g
- Sodium: 300-400mg

NOTES

RATING

DIFFICULTY

Chicken Alfredo

PREP 15 MIN

COOK 25 MIN

4 SERVES

Benefits of Chicken Alfredo

Olive Oil: A good source of monounsaturated fats.

Promotes heart health.

Garlic: Offers anti-inflammatory and antioxidant benefits.

To support immune system.

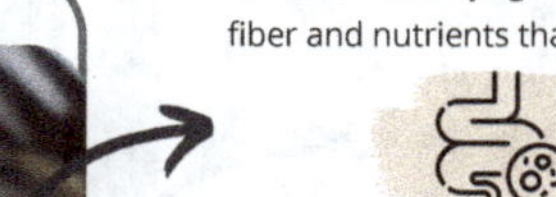

Whole Wheat Spaghetti: Offers more fiber and nutrients than regular pasta.

Aids digestion.

Chicken: Provides high-quality protein. Rich in various vitamins and minerals, including B vitamins.

To grow and repair muscles. For energy production.

Ingredients & Tools

For the Chicken:

- 2 boneless, skinless chicken breasts
- Salt and pepper to taste
- 1 tablespoon olive oil

For the Alfredo Sauce:

- 1 tablespoon unsalted butter
- 1 clove garlic, minced
- 1 cup heavy cream (use light cream or half-and-half for a lighter version)
- 1 cup grated Parmesan cheese (use reduced-fat cheese if available)
- Salt and pepper to taste
- For the Pasta:
- 8 ounces fettuccine or your choice of pasta (use whole wheat pasta for added fiber)

Additional:

- Chopped parsley for garnish
- Extra Parmesan cheese for serving

Tips for Success

Sauce Consistency: Be careful not to let the sauce boil vigorously after adding the cheese to prevent the sauce from separating and becoming grainy.

Serving Suggestion: For added vegetables, toss in some steamed broccoli or spinach when combining the pasta with the sauce.

It is recommended to enjoy Chicken Alfredo in moderation, especially if managing dietary fat intake, as it has high calorie and fat content.

METHOD

Step 1: Cook the Pasta:
Bring a large pot of salted water to a boil. Add the pasta and cook according to package instructions until al dente. Drain and set aside, reserving some pasta water.

Step 2: Season the chicken breasts with salt and pepper. Heat the olive oil in a skillet over medium-high heat.
Cook the chicken until golden and cooked through, about 6-7 minutes per side depending on thickness. Transfer to a cutting board, let rest for a few minutes, then slice.

Step 3: In the same skillet, reduce heat to medium and add the butter. Once melted, add the minced garlic and sauté for about 1 minute until fragrant. Pour in the cream and bring to a simmer. Add the grated Parmesan cheese and stir until the sauce thickens, about 5 minutes. Season with salt and pepper to taste.If the sauce is too thick, add a little reserved pasta water.

Step 4: Toss the cooked pasta with the Alfredo sauce you made, coating the noodles thoroughly. Plate the pasta, top with sliced chicken, and garnish with chopped parsley and extra Parmesan cheese.

Per Serving:

- Calories: 500-550
- Protein: 30-35g
- Fat: 25-30g
- Carbohydrates: 40-45g
- Fiber: 2-3g
- Sodium: 600-700mg

NOTES

RATING

DIFFICULTY

Pork Chops

PREP 10 MIN

COOK 20 MIN

4 SERVES

Benefits of Pork Chops

Pork Chops: Provide high-quality protein and essential nutrients like B vitamins (particularly B1, B6, and B12)

To stay smart.

For energy production.

Olive Oil: A good source of monounsaturated fats

Promotes heart health.

Apple Cider and Vinegar: Both contain acetic acid, which has been shown to help lower blood sugar levels post-meal

For longer feeling of fullness.

Ingredients & Tools

For the Pork Chops:

- 4 bone-in pork chops (about 1 inch thick)
- Salt and pepper to taste
- 2 tablespoons olive oil
- 2 cloves garlic, minced
- 1 teaspoon dried thyme or rosemary (or a combination)

For the Apple Cider Glaze:

- 1 cup apple cider
- 1 tablespoon Dijon mustard
- 1 tablespoon honey
- 1 tablespoon apple cider vinegar
- Salt and pepper to taste
- **Additional:**
- Fresh herbs for garnish (such as thyme or parsley)

Tips for Success

Don't Overcook: To ensure the pork chops are juicy and tender, avoid overcooking. The pork is safe to eat at 145°F, which will leave it slightly pink in the center.

Resting Time: Let the pork chops rest for 3-5 minutes after cooking. This helps the juices redistribute throughout the meat, making it more tender and flavorful.

It is recommended to consider portion sizes and frequency of consumption if managing dietary intake. Pair the pork chops with a side of steamed vegetables and a whole grain like quinoa or brown rice for a well-rounded meal.

METHOD

Step 1: Season both sides of the pork chops with salt, pepper, and dried herbs. Heat olive oil in a large skillet over medium-high heat. Add the pork chops and cook for about 4-5 minutes per side, or until they reach an internal temperature of 145°F (63°C) and are golden brown. Remove from the skillet and set aside to rest.

Step 2: Make the Apple Cider Glaze: In the same skillet, reduce heat to medium. Add the minced garlic and sauté for about 1 minute until fragrant. Add the apple cider, Dijon mustard, honey, and apple cider vinegar. Stir to combine and bring to a simmer.

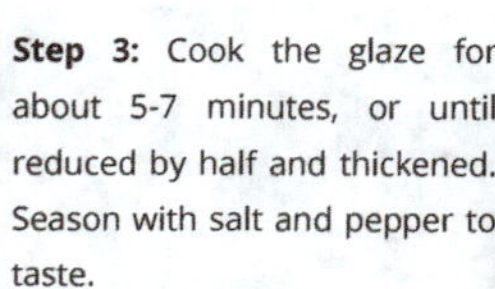

Step 3: Cook the glaze for about 5-7 minutes, or until reduced by half and thickened. Season with salt and pepper to taste.

Step 4: Spoon the apple cider glaze over the cooked pork chops. Garnish with fresh herbs if desired.

Per Serving:

- Calories: 350-400
- Protein: 35-40g
- Fat: 20-25g
- Carbohydrates: 10-15g
- Fiber: 0-1g
- Sodium: 300-400mg

NOTES

RATING

DIFFICULTY

Teriyaki Chicken

PREP 15 MIN

COOK 20 MIN

4 SERVES

Benefits of Teriyaki Chicken

Chicken: Provides high-quality protein. Rich in various vitamins and minerals, including B vitamins.

To grow and repair muscles. For energy production.

Garlic : Offers anti-inflammatory and antioxidant benefits.

To support immune system.

Honey: Offers antioxidants, though it is high in sugars, so should be used moderately.

Promotes heart health.

Soy Sauce: Contains trace minerals like manganese and selenium but should be used in low-sodium versions to reduce salt intake.

For strong bones and teeth.

Ingredients & Tools

For the Chicken:

- 1 1/2 pounds boneless, skinless chicken thighs or breasts pieces
- 1 tablespoon olive oil

For the Teriyaki Sauce:

- 1/3 cup low-sodium soy sauce
- 3 tablespoons honey (or a reduced amount to lower sugar content)
- 2 cloves garlic, minced
- 1 tablespoon freshly grated ginger
- 1 tablespoon rice vinegar
- 1 tablespoon cornstarch dissolved in 2 tablespoons water to make a slurry

Additional:

- Sesame seeds for garnish
- Sliced green onions for garnish
- Steamed broccoli or mixed vegetables for serving
- Cooked brown rice or quinoa for serving

Tips for Success

Sauce Thickness: Adjust the thickness of the sauce by varying the amount of cornstarch slurry based on your preference.

Avoid Overcooking: Keep an eye on the chicken to ensure it doesn't overcook, as chicken thighs can become tough if cooked too long.

It is recommended to be mindful of portion sizes, especially with the sauce, as it contains honey and soy sauce, which are high in sugars and sodium.

METHOD

Step 1: Prepare the Teriyaki Sauce:
In a small bowl, whisk together soy sauce, honey, garlic, ginger, and rice vinegar. Set the cornstarch slurry aside for later use.

Step 2: Cook the Chicken:
Heat olive oil in a large skillet over medium-high heat. Add the chicken thighs and cook for about 5-6 minutes on each side until nicely browned and nearly cooked through. Reduce heat to medium.

Step 3: Add the Sauce:
Pour the teriyaki sauce mixture over the chicken in the skillet. Allow to simmer for a few minutes, letting the sauce reduce slightly. Add the cornstarch slurry, stirring constantly, until the sauce thickens to a glossy finish that coats the chicken.

Step 4:
Once the chicken is thoroughly cooked and the sauce is thickened, remove from heat. Slice the chicken, if desired, and serve over cooked brown rice or quinoa. Garnish with sesame seeds and green onions. Serve steamed broccoli or a mix of vegetables on the side.

Per Serving:

- Calories: 300-350
- Protein: 25-30g
- Fat: 10-15g
- Carbohydrates: 20-25g
- Fiber: 1-2g
- Sodium: 600-700mg

NOTES

RATING

DIFFICULTY

Chicken Pot Pie

PREP 30 MIN

COOK 30 MIN

6 SERVES

Benefits of Chicken Pot Pie

Chicken: Provides high-quality protein. Rich in various vitamins and minerals, including B vitamins.

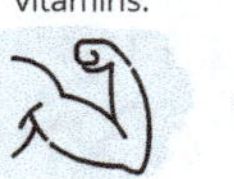

To grow and repair muscles. For energy production.

Whole Wheat Flour: Higher in fiber than white flour.

Provides a slower release of energy.

Vegetables: Carrots, celery, and peas offer vitamins, minerals, fiber, and antioxidants.

To support immune system.

Aid digestive system.

Ingredients & Tools

For the Filling:

- 2 tablespoons olive oil
- 1 large onion, chopped
- 2 carrots, peeled and diced
- 2 celery stalks, diced
- 3 cups cooked chicken, shredded (preferably from a rotisserie chicken or leftover roasted chicken)
- 1/3 cup all-purpose flour (substitute with whole wheat flour for a healthier option)
- 1 1/2 cups low-sodium chicken broth
- 1 cup milk (opt for skim milk)
- 1 cup frozen peas
- 1 teaspoon dried thyme
- Salt and pepper to taste

For the Crust:

- 1 package (about 14-16 ounces) refrigerated pie dough (use a whole wheat crust if available)
- 1 egg, beaten for egg wash

Tips for Success

Making Ahead: The filling can be made ahead and stored in the refrigerator for up to two days, which can help intensify the flavors.

Dough Tip: If the pie crust browns too quickly, cover the edges with aluminum foil during baking.

It is recommended to be mindful of portion sizes, especially due to the richness of the pie crust and filling. Serve with a side salad or additional steamed vegetables.

METHOD

Step 1: Prepare the Filling:
Heat the olive oil in a large skillet or saucepan over medium heat. Add the onion, carrots, and celery, and cook until the vegetables are softened, about 5-7 minutes. Stir in the flour and cook for 1 minute to remove the raw flour taste.

Step 2: Gradually add the chicken broth and milk, stirring continuously until the mixture is smooth and begins to thicken. Add the shredded chicken, frozen peas, thyme, salt, and pepper. Cook until the peas are heated through and the mixture is thick, about 5 minutes. Remove from heat.

Step 3: Preheat your oven to 375°F (190°C). Roll out the pie dough and fit one piece into a 9-inch pie dish. Spoon the filling into the pie crust. Cover with the second piece of dough. Seal the edges and trim any excess dough. Make several small slits in the top crust to allow steam to escape. Brush the top crust with beaten egg to get a golden finish.

Step 4: Place the pie in the oven and bake for 30-35 minutes or until the crust is golden brown and the filling is bubbly. Let the pie cool for 10 minutes before serving.

Per Serving:

- Calories: 400-450
- Protein: 25-30g
- Fat: 20-25g
- Carbohydrates: 30-35g
- Fiber: 3-4g
- Sodium: 600-700mg

NOTES

RATING

DIFFICULTY

Shepherd's Pie

PREP 30 MIN

COOK 30 MIN

6 SERVES

Benefits of Shepherd's Pie

Lamb/Beef: Provides high-quality protein and essential nutrients like iron, zinc, and B vitamins.

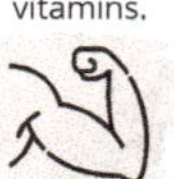

To grow and repair muscles. For energy production.

Potatoes: Are a good source of vitamin C, potassium, and dietary fiber.

Aid in digestion.

Carrots and Peas: Offer beta-carotene, vitamins, and fiber which are vital for health and well-being.

To support immune system.

Olive Oil: A good source of monounsaturated fats.

Promotes heart health.

Ingredients & Tools

For the Meat Filling:

- 1 tablespoon olive oil
- 1 large onion, finely chopped
- 2 carrots, peeled and diced
- 2 cloves garlic, minced
- 1 lb ground lamb (traditionally used) or ground beef (for a Cottage Pie variation)
- 2 tablespoons tomato paste
- 1 cup beef or vegetable broth
- 1 teaspoon Worcestershire sauce
- 1 teaspoon dried thyme
- 1/2 cup frozen peas
- Salt and pepper to taste
- For the Mashed Potato Topping:
- 2 pounds potatoes, peeled and cut into chunks
- 1/4 cup milk (use skim milk for a lighter version)
- 2 tablespoons unsalted butter (or use a butter substitute for lower fat)
- Salt and pepper to taste

Tips for Success

Enhancing Flavor: For deeper flavor, you can add a splash of red wine to the meat mixture while cooking.

Broiler Finish: For a crispier top, place the pie under the broiler for the last few minutes until browned to your liking.

It is recommended to be mindful of portion sizes as this dish is quite hearty and rich. Serve with a side of steamed green vegetables like broccoli or Brussels sprouts to round out the meal.

METHOD

Step 1: Boil the potatoes in salted water until tender, about 15-20 minutes. Drain well and mash with milk, butter, salt, and pepper until smooth and creamy. Set aside.

Step 2: Make the Meat Filling: Heat the olive oil in a large skillet over medium heat. Add the onion and carrots, cooking until softened, about 5 minutes. Add the garlic and ground meat, breaking it up with a spoon, and brown until no pink remains.

Step 3: Stir in the tomato paste, broth, Worcestershire sauce, and thyme. Simmer until the juices thicken, about 10 minutes. Add the frozen peas and cook for another 2-3 minutes. Season with salt and pepper to taste. Transfer the meat mixture to a baking dish.

Step 4: Preheat your oven to 400°F (200°C). Spoon the mashed potatoes over the meat filling, spreading evenly. Use a fork to create ridges on top. Bake in the preheated oven for about 20 minutes or until the top is golden and the edges are bubbly. Let the Shepherd's Pie sit for 10 minutes before serving to set up a bit. Garnish with fresh herbs.

Per Serving:

- Calories: 400-450
- Protein: 25-30g
- Fat: 20-25g
- Carbohydrates: 35-40g
- Fiber: 5-6g
- Sodium: 300-400mg

NOTES

RATING

DIFFICULTY

Chili

PREP 20 MIN
COOK 60 MIN
6 SERVES

Benefits of Chili

Lean Protein: Both ground beef and turkey provide high-quality protein.

To grow and repair muscles. For energy production.

Beans: High in fiber, protein, and iron. They also provide a good source of complex carbohydrates.

Aid in digestion.

Tomatoes: Rich in vitamin C, potassium, folate, and vitamin K, and a great source of antioxidants, including lycopene.

Promotes heart health.

Spices: Chili powder, cumin, and paprika contain antioxidants that help reduce inflammation and boost metabolism.

To support immune system.

Ingredients & Tools

For the Chili:

- 2 tablespoons olive oil
- 1 large onion, chopped
- 2 cloves garlic, minced
- 1 bell pepper, any color, diced
- 1 lb ground beef or turkey (use turkey for a leaner option)
- 2 tablespoons chili powder
- 1 teaspoon cumin
- 1 teaspoon smoked paprika
- 1/2 teaspoon cayenne pepper (optional)
- 1 can (28 ounces) crushed tomatoes
- 1 can (15 ounces) kidney beans, drained and rinsed
- 1 cup beef or vegetable broth (use low sodium)
- Salt and pepper to taste

Additional:

- Chopped green onions, shredded cheese (use low-fat cheese), and sour cream (use low-fat or Greek yogurt) for garnish

Tips for Success

Slow Cooking: For deeper flavor development, let the chili simmer slowly on low heat for a longer period, or use a slow cooker.

Flavor Enhancers: Consider adding a bit of dark chocolate or coffee grounds to the chili for added depth and complexity.

It is recommended to watch portion sizes to manage calorie intake effectively. Complement the chili with a side of cornbread and a fresh salad for a balanced meal.

METHOD

Step 1: Prepare the Base:
Heat olive oil in a large pot over medium heat. Add the onion, garlic, and bell pepper. Sauté until soft and translucent, about 5-7 minutes. Add the ground beef or turkey. Cook until browned, breaking up the meat with a spoon, about 8-10 minutes.

Step 2: Add Spices and Tomatoes: Stir in the chili powder, cumin, smoked paprika, and cayenne pepper. Cook for another minute until fragrant. Pour in the crushed tomatoes and broth. Stir to combine.

Step 3: Simmer:
Bring the mixture to a boil, then reduce heat to low and simmer, partially covered, for about 45-50 minutes. The chili should thicken and flavors meld.

Step 4: Add Beans: Add the kidney beans and cook for another 10 minutes. Adjust seasoning with salt and pepper. Serve hot, garnished with green onions, shredded cheese, and a dollop of sour cream or Greek yogurt.

Per Serving:

- Calories: 350-400
- Protein: 25-30g
- Fat: 15-20g
- Carbohydrates: 20-25g
- Fiber: 6-7g
- Sodium: 300-400mg

NOTES

RATING

DIFFICULTY

Jambalaya

PREP 20 MIN

COOK 40 MIN

6 SERVES

Benefits of Jambalaya

Chicken and Shrimp: Provide high-quality protein. **Turkey Sausage:** A healthier alternative to traditional sausage, reducing fat content.

To grow and repair muscles. For energy production.

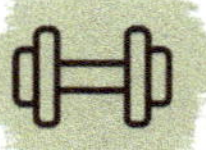

to stay fit and healthy.

Tomatoes and Bell Peppers: Rich in vitamins C and A, potassium, and fiber. They also contain antioxidants that help combat free radicals.

Promotes heart health.

Garlic and Onions: thanks to their natural antioxidant properties.

support immune system.

Ingredients & Tools

For the Jambalaya:

- 2 tablespoons olive oil
- 1 lb chicken breast, cut into bite-sized pieces
- 8 ounces andouille sausage, sliced (use turkey sausage for a leaner option)
- 1 large onion, chopped
- 1 green bell pepper, chopped
- 3 celery stalks, chopped
- 2 cloves garlic, minced
- 1 can (14.5 ounces) diced tomatoes
- 1 teaspoon smoked paprika
- 1 teaspoon dried thyme
- 1/2 teaspoon cayenne pepper
- 1/2 teaspoon salt
- 1/4 teaspoon black pepper
- 2 cups low-sodium chicken broth
- 1 cup long-grain rice
- 1 lb shrimp, peeled and deveined

Additional:

- Chopped parsley for garnish
- Slices of lemon for serving

Tips for Success

Rice Consistency: Ensure the rice is submerged in the liquid for even cooking. Adjust liquid if necessary.

Seafood Addition: Add the shrimp toward the end of cooking to prevent overcooking.

It is recommended to adjust the level of cayenne pepper according to your heat preference, keeping in mind that the flavors intensify as they cook. Serve with a side of steamed green vegetables, such as broccoli or green beans, to balance out the meal.

METHOD

Step 1: Cook the Meats:
Heat olive oil in a large pot or Dutch oven over medium-high heat. Add the copped onion, the chicken pieces and sausage slices. Cook until the chicken is browned and the sausage is slightly crispy, about 5-7 minutes. Remove with a slotted spoon and set aside.

Step 2: Sauté Vegetables: In the same pot add bell pepper, and celery. Cook until the vegetables are softened, about 5 minutes. Add garlic, paprika, thyme, cayenne pepper, salt, and black pepper. Cook for an additional 2 minutes until fragrant.

Step 3: Add Rice and Liquids:
Stir in the diced tomatoes and chicken broth, scraping any browned bits off the bottom of the pot. Add the rice and bring the mixture to a boil.

Step 4: Reduce heat to low, cover, and simmer for 20 minutes, or until the rice is almost tender. Stir in the shrimp and the reserved chicken and sausage. Cover and cook for another 10 minutes, or until the shrimp are pink. Remove from heat and let sit, covered, for 5 minutes.Garnish with chopped parsley and serve with lemon slices.

Per Serving:

- Calories: 450-500
- Protein: 35-40g
- Fat: 15-20g
- Carbohydrates: 35-40g
- Fiber: 3-4g
- Sodium: 600-700mg

NOTES

RATING

DIFFICULTY

Chicken Curry

PREP 15 MIN

COOK 30 MIN

4 SERVES

Benefits of Chicken Curry

Chicken: Provide high-quality protein

to grow and repair muscles. For energy production.

Coconut Milk: Provides healthy fats

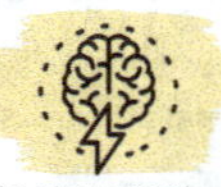

to stay smart.

Tomatoes: Rich in vitamin C, potassium, folate, and vitamin K, and a great source of antioxidants, including lycopene.

Promotes heart health

Onion, Garlic and Ginger: Rich in antioxidants and have antibacterial properties

To support immune system.

Ingredients & Tools

- 1 lb (450g) boneless, skinless chicken breast - cut into bite-sized pieces
- 1 onion - finely chopped
- 2 garlic cloves - minced
- 1-inch piece of ginger - minced
- 1 can (14 oz) of diced tomatoes
- 1 can (14 oz) of coconut milk
- 2 tbsp curry powder
- 1 tsp ground cumin
- 1 tsp ground coriander
- 1/2 tsp turmeric powder
- 1/4 tsp cayenne pepper (optional for a bit of heat)
- 2 tbsp vegetable oil
- Salt and pepper to taste
- Fresh cilantro - chopped, for garnish
- Cooked rice or naan bread - for serving

Tips for Success

Adjust the Heat: If you prefer a milder curry, omit the cayenne pepper.

Fresh Spices: Use fresh spices for the best flavor. Ground spices lose their potency over time.

It is recommended to stick to the serving size to avoid overeating. Incorporate a variety of vegetables into the curry, like bell peppers, spinach, or peas, for added nutrients.

METHOD

Step 1: Cook the prepared Onion, Garlic, and Ginger: Heat the oil in a large pan over medium heat. Add the chopped onion and sauté until golden brown, about 5 minutes. Add the minced garlic and ginger, and cook for another 1-2 minutes.

Step 2: Stir in the curry powder, ground cumin, ground coriander, turmeric, and cayenne pepper (if using). Cook for 1 minute until fragrant. Add the chicken pieces to the pan, season with salt and pepper, and cook until the chicken is no longer pink on the outside, about 5-7 minutes.

Step 3: Add Tomatoes and Coconut Milk:
Pour in the diced tomatoes (with their juice) and coconut milk.
Bring to a simmer and cook for 15-20 minutes until the chicken is cooked through and the sauce has thickened.

Step 4: Taste and adjust the seasoning with salt and pepper if needed. Garnish with fresh chopped cilantro. Serve hot over cooked rice or with naan bread.

Per Serving:

- Calories: 350
- Protein: 25g
- Carbohydrates: 10g
- Fat: 23g
- Fiber: 3g
- Sugar: 6g

NOTES

RATING

DIFFICULTY

BBQ Pulled Pork

PREP 15 MIN

COOK 2-3 HOURS

8-10 SERVES

Benefits of BBQ Pulled Pork

Pork Shoulder: High in protein. Contains vitamins and minerals like B vitamins and zinc.

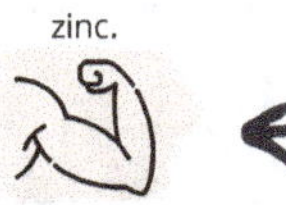

To grow and repair muscles. For energy production.

Whole burger buns: Higher in fiber than regular buns

Provides a slower release of energy.

Worcestershire sauce contains Vinegar, small amounts of vitamins and minerals like vitamin B6, vitamin C, iron, and niacin, contributing to overall nutrition.

Aid in digestion.

Onion and Spices: Rich in antioxidants , anti-inflammatory properties.

To support immune system.

Ingredients & Tools

- 3-4 lbs (1.4-1.8 kg) pork shoulder (pork butt)
- 1 large onion - sliced
- 4 garlic cloves - minced
- 1 cup BBQ sauce
- 1/2 cup apple cider vinegar
- 1/2 cup chicken broth
- 1/4 cup brown sugar
- 1 tbsp Worcestershire sauce
- 1 tbsp yellow mustard
- 1 tsp smoked paprika
- 1 tsp chili powder
- 1/2 tsp black pepper
- 1/2 tsp salt
- 1/4 tsp cayenne pepper (optional for a bit of heat)
- Burger buns - for serving
- Coleslaw - for serving (optional)

Tips for Success

Brown the Meat: Browning the pork adds extra flavor to the dish.

Low and Slow: Keep the heat low and cook the pork slowly for the best texture.

Flavor Boost: Add more BBQ sauce after shredding for extra flavor.

It is recommended to stick to the serving size to avoid overeating. Pair with a side of vegetables or a fresh salad for a balanced meal.

METHOD

Step 1: Brown the Pork:
Heat a large pot or Dutch oven over medium-high heat. Season the pork shoulder with salt and pepper. Add a bit of oil to the pot and brown the pork on all sides (about 2-3 minutes per side). Remove the pork and set it aside.

Step 2: Cook the Onion:
In the same pot, add the sliced onion and cook until softened, about 5 minutes. In a bowl, combine BBQ sauce, apple cider vinegar, chicken broth, brown sugar, Worcestershire sauce, mustard, smoked paprika, and chili powder.

Step 3: Cook the Pork:
Return the pork to the pot, pour the sauce mixture over it, and bring to a simmer.
Reduce the heat to low, cover, and let it cook for 2-3 hours, or until the pork is tender and easily shredded with a fork.

Step 4: Shred the Pork:
Remove the pork from the pot and shred it using two forks.
Return the shredded pork to the pot and mix it with the sauce.
Serve:
Serve the BBQ pulled pork on burger buns with coleslaw if desired.

Per Serving:

- Calories: 400
- Protein: 30g
- Carbohydrates: 25g
- Fat: 20g
- Fiber: 1g
- Sugar: 15g

NOTES

RATING

DIFFICULTY

Stuffed Bell Peppers

PREP 15 MIN

COOK 45 MIN

6 SERVES

Benefits of Stuffed Bell Peppers

Bell Peppers: High in vitamins A and C, antioxidants, and fiber.

Aid in digestion.

Tomatoes: Rich in vitamin C, potassium, folate, and vitamin K, and a great source of antioxidants, including lycopene.

Promote heart health.

Ground Beef/Turkey: Excellent source of protein. Turkey is a leaner option.

To grow and repair muscles. For energy production.

Rice: Provides energy through carbohydrates and contains some essential vitamins and minerals.

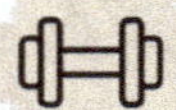

to stay fit and healthy.

Ingredients & Tools

- 6 large bell peppers (any color)
- 1 lb (450g) ground beef or turkey
- 1 cup cooked rice (white or brown)
- 1 can (14.5 oz) diced tomatoes (drained)
- 1 small onion - finely chopped
- 2 cloves garlic - minced
- 1 cup shredded cheese (cheddar or mozzarella)
- 1 tsp dried oregano
- 1 tsp dried basil
- Salt and pepper to taste
- 1 tbsp olive oil
- 1 cup tomato sauce (for topping)
- Fresh parsley - chopped, for garnish

Tips for Success

Even Cooking: Boil the peppers briefly to ensure they cook evenly in the oven.

Flavor Adjustment: Adjust seasonings to your taste, adding more herbs or spices as desired.

Cheese Variety: Use your favorite cheese or a blend of cheeses for a different flavor profile.

It is recommended to stick to one stuffed pepper per serving to manage calorie intake. Choose lean ground turkey for a lower-fat option. Use brown rice instead of white rice for added fiber and nutrients. Pair with a side salad or steamed vegetables for a balanced meal.

METHOD

Step 1: Preheat Oven:

Preheat your oven to 375°F (190°C).

Cut the tops off the bell peppers and remove the seeds and membranes.

Place the bell peppers in a large pot of boiling water for 5 minutes to soften. Remove and drain.

Step 2: Cook the Filling:

In a large skillet, heat the olive oil over medium heat.

Add the chopped onion and garlic, and cook until softened, about 5 minutes.

Add the ground beef (or turkey) and cook until browned, breaking it up with a spoon as it cooks.

Step 3: Stir in the cooked rice, diced tomatoes, oregano, basil, salt, and pepper. Cook for another 5 minutes to combine the flavors. Fill each bell pepper with the meat and rice mixture. Place the stuffed peppers in a baking dish. Pour the tomato sauce over the top of the peppers.

Step 4: Cover the baking dish with aluminum foil and bake for 30 minutes. Remove the foil, sprinkle the shredded cheese on top of each pepper, and bake for an additional 10-15 minutes, or until the cheese is melted and bubbly. Garnish with fresh chopped parsley before serving.

Per Serving:

- Calories: 350
- Protein: 25g
- Carbohydrates: 30g
- Fat: 15g
- Fiber: 4g
- Sugar: 8g

NOTES

RATING

DIFFICULTY

Baked Salmon

PREP 10 MIN

COOK 20 MIN

4 SERVES

Benefits of Baked Salmon

Salmon: High in omega-3 fatty acids. Rich in high-quality protein and B vitamins.
Lemon: High in vitamin C.

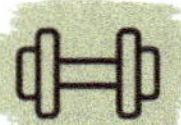

To stay fit and healthy.

Olive Oil: Contains healthy monounsaturated fats and antioxidants

Promotes heart health.

Dill: Rich in antioxidants and provides vitamins A and C

For eye health.

Garlic: Contains compounds with potent medicinal properties, such as allicin has antibacterial effects.

To support immune system.

Ingredients & Tools

- 4 salmon fillets (6 oz each)
- 2 tbsp olive oil
- 1 lemon - thinly sliced
- 2 cloves garlic - minced
- 1 tbsp fresh dill - chopped (or 1 tsp dried dill)
- Salt and pepper to taste
- 1/2 tsp paprika (optional for extra flavor)
- Fresh parsley - chopped, for garnish

Tips for Success

Check Doneness: Use a meat thermometer to ensure the salmon is cooked to the right temperature.

Flavor Variations: Experiment with different herbs and spices, such as thyme, rosemary, or chili flakes.

Easy Cleanup: Use foil or parchment paper to make cleanup a breeze.

It is recommended to stick to the recommended serving size to manage calorie intake. Pair with a side of steamed vegetables or a fresh salad for a balanced meal. The omega-3 fatty acids in salmon are beneficial for heart health, so include fatty fish in your diet regularly.

METHOD

Step 1: Preheat Oven:
Preheat your oven to 400°F (200°C). Line a baking sheet with aluminum foil or parchment paper for easy cleanup.
Lightly grease the foil with a bit of olive oil to prevent sticking.

Step 2: Season the Salmon:
Place the salmon fillets on the prepared baking sheet.
Drizzle the olive oil over the fillets.
Sprinkle the minced garlic, chopped dill, salt, pepper, and paprika evenly over the salmon.
Place the lemon slices on top of and around the salmon fillets.

Step 3: Bake in the preheated oven for 15-20 minutes, or until the salmon is opaque and flakes easily with a fork. The internal temperature should reach 145°F (63°C).

Step 4: Garnish and Serve: Garnish with fresh chopped parsley before serving.

Per Serving:

- Calories: 300
- Protein: 34g
- Carbohydrates: 2g
- Fat: 18g
- Fiber: 1g
- Sugar: 0g

NOTES

RATING

DIFFICULTY

Chicken and Dumplings

PREP 20 MIN

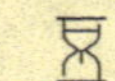
COOK 40 MIN

6 SERVES

Benefits of Chicken and Dumplings

Chicken: Provides high-quality protein.

To grow and repair muscles. For energy production.

Using whole flour which is higher in fiber.

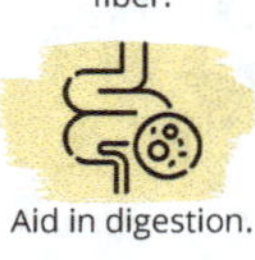

Aid in digestion.

Vegetables: Carrots and celery offer fiber, vitamins, and minerals .

For energy production.

To stay smart.

To support immune system.

Ingredients & Tools

For the Chicken Stew:

- 2 tablespoons olive oil
- 1 large onion, chopped
- 2 carrots, peeled and diced
- 2 celery stalks, diced
- 3 cloves garlic, minced
- 1 lb boneless, skinless chicken breasts or thighs, diced
- 6 cups low-sodium chicken broth
- 1 teaspoon dried thyme
- 1 bay leaf
- Salt and pepper to taste
- 1/2 cup heavy cream

For the Dumplings:

- 2 cups all-purpose flour
- 1 tablespoon baking powder
- 1/2 teaspoon salt
- 2 tablespoons butter, melted
- 1 cup milk

Tips for Success

Dumpling Consistency: Be careful not to overmix the dumpling batter, as it can make the dumplings tough.

Simmering: Keep the stew at a gentle simmer when cooking the dumplings to ensure they cook evenly without falling apart.

It is recommended that if you are using cream, consider the added calories and fat. Opting for low-fat milk can reduce these without sacrificing too much flavor.

METHOD

Step 1: Prepare the Chicken Stew:
Heat the olive oil in a large pot over medium heat. Add the onion, carrots, celery, and garlic. Cook until the vegetables are softened, about 5-7 minutes. Add the chicken breasts or thighs to the pot. Pour in the chicken broth, then add the thyme, bay leaf, salt, and pepper.

Step 2: Bring to a boil, then reduce heat to a simmer. Cover and cook until the chicken is cooked through, about 20 minutes. Remove the chicken, shred it, and return it to the pot. Stir in the cream or milk if using and adjust seasoning.

Step 3: In a mixing bowl, combine the flour, baking powder, and salt. Add the melted butter and milk to the dry ingredients. Stir until the mixture just comes together; do not overmix. Drop tablespoon-sized dollops of the dumpling dough into the simmering stew. Cover the pot and let the dumplings cook for 15-20 minutes until they are puffy and firm.

Step 4: Finish and Serve:
Once the dumplings are cooked, discard the bay leaf. Serve the chicken and dumplings hot, garnished with fresh parsley if desired.

Per Serving:

- Calories: 350-400
- Protein: 25-30g
- Fat: 15-20g
- Carbohydrates: 30-35g
- Fiber: 3-4g
- Sodium: 300-400mg

NOTES

RATING

DIFFICULTY

Sloppy Joe Casserole

PREP 20 MIN

COOK 20 MIN

6 SERVES

Benefits of Sloppy Joe Casserole

Whole Grains: Opting for a whole grain cornbread mix can increase fiber content.

Aid in digestion

For energy production

Vegetables: Onion and bell pepper add fiber, vitamins A and C, and antioxidants.

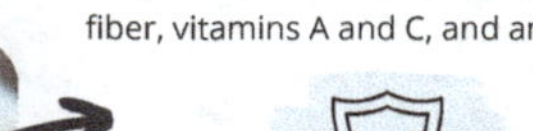

To support immune system

Lean Meat: Using ground turkey instead of beef provides a lower fat option that's still high in protein.

To grow and repair muscles. For energy production

Ingredients & Tools

- 1 tablespoon olive oil
- 1 onion, finely chopped
- 1 bell pepper, finely chopped
- 2 cloves garlic, minced
- 1 lb ground beef or turkey
- 1 can (15 oz) tomato sauce
- 2 tablespoons tomato paste
- 1 tablespoon Worcestershire sauce
- 1 tablespoon mustard
- 2 tablespoons brown sugar
- Salt and pepper to taste

For the Topping:

- 1 package (8.5 oz) cornbread mix (prepare according to package instructions)
- 1 egg (as called for by the cornbread mix)
- 1/3 cup milk (as called for by the cornbread mix)

Additional:

- 1 cup shredded cheddar cheese
- Chopped parsley for garnish

Tips for Success

Sauce Thickness: Ensure the filling is thick enough before baking to prevent it from making the cornbread soggy.

Keep an eye on the casserole in the oven, especially towards the end of baking. Cornbread can go from perfectly golden to overly browned fairly quickly.

It is recommended to consider serving smaller portions, especially if it's part of a meal with multiple dishes. Sloppy Joe Casserole can be quite filling and rich in calories. Serve the casserole with a side of steamed vegetables, like broccoli, carrots, green beans, or a fresh green salad.

METHOD

Step 1: Heat olive oil in a large skillet over medium heat. Add onion, bell pepper, and garlic. Cook until softened, about 5 minutes. Add the ground meat. Cook until browned. Drain any excess fat. Stir in tomato sauce, tomato paste, Worcestershire sauce, mustard, and brown sugar. Simmer for about 10 minutes until thickened. Season with salt and pepper.

Step 2: Prepare the Cornbread Topping: While the filling simmers, prepare the cornbread batter according to the package instructions, using the specified amounts of egg and milk.

Step 3: Assemble the Casserole: Preheat the oven to 375°F (190°C). Spread the Sloppy Joe filling evenly in a 9x13 inch baking dish. Sprinkle half of the shredded cheese over the filling. Pour the cornbread batter over the top, spreading gently to cover. Sprinkle the remaining cheese on top of the cornbread batter.

Step 4: Place in the oven and bake for 15-20 minutes, or until the cornbread topping is cooked through and golden. Let the casserole cool slightly before serving. Garnish with chopped parsley if desired.

Per Serving:

- Calories: 450-500
- Protein: 25-30g
- Fat: 20-25g
- Carbohydrates: 40-45g
- Fiber: 3-4g
- Sodium: 600-700mg

NOTES

RATING

DIFFICULTY

Goulash

PREP 15 MIN | COOK 2 HOURS | 6 SERVES

Benefits of Goulash

Vegetables: Onions, bell peppers, and tomatoes are high in vitamins C and K, fiber, and antioxidants.

Promotes heart health.

Potatoes: Offer vitamin C, potassium, and dietary fiber.

Aid in digestion.

Paprika: Rich in antioxidants, including vitamin A.

To support immune system.

For eye health.

Beef: Provides high-quality protein and essential nutrients like iron and zinc

To grow and repair muscles. For energy production.

Ingredients & Tools

For the Goulash:

- 2 tablespoons olive oil
- 2 large onions, chopped
- 2 cloves garlic, minced
- 2 tablespoons sweet paprika (Hungarian if available)
- 1 teaspoon caraway seeds
- 1.5 pounds beef chuck, cut into 1-inch cubes
- 1 red bell pepper, diced
- 1 green bell pepper, diced
- 2 tomatoes, peeled and chopped, or 1 can (14 oz) diced tomatoes
- 2 cups beef broth (low sodium)
- 1 teaspoon salt
- 1/2 teaspoon black pepper
- 1 bay leaf
- 2 medium potatoes, peeled and cubed

Tips for Success

Proper Paprika: Use authentic Hungarian paprika if possible, as it offers a distinctive sweet and earthy flavor that is traditional to Goulash.

Slow Cooking: Letting the goulash simmer slowly helps develop deep, rich flavors and ensures the meat is tender.

Thickening the Stew: If the goulash is too liquid, you can simmer it uncovered in the last 30 minutes to reduce and thicken the sauce.

It is recommended to enjoy it in moderation, particularly if watching calorie intake. Despite its nutritional benefits, goulash is rich and hearty. Pair the goulash with a side of crusty bread for dipping and a fresh green salad to balance out the richness of the stew.

METHOD

Step 1: Sauté Onions and Spices: Heat olive oil in a large pot or Dutch oven over medium heat. Add onions and garlic, sautéing until onions are translucent, about 5 minutes. Stir in paprika and caraway seeds, cooking for another minute until fragrant.

Step 2: Brown the Beef: Increase heat to medium-high and add the beef cubes to the pot. Brown the meat on all sides. Add the diced bell peppers, tomatoes, beef broth, salt, pepper, and bay leaf.
Bring to a boil, then reduce heat to low, cover, and simmer for about 1.5 hours.

Step 3: Add Potatoes: After the beef has simmered, add the cubed potatoes and continue to simmer covered for another 30 minutes, or until the potatoes are tender and the stew has thickened.

Step 4: Finish and Serve: Remove the bay leaf and adjust seasoning as needed. Serve hot, garnished with fresh parsley or a dollop of sour cream if desired.

Per Serving:

- Calories: 350-400
- Protein: 25-30g
- Fat: 20-25g
- Carbohydrates: 15-20g
- Fiber: 3-4g
- Sodium: 300-400mg

NOTES

RATING

DIFFICULTY

Stir Fry

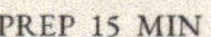
PREP 15 MIN

COOK 10 MIN

4 SERVES

Healthy Fats: Using oils like olive or avocado provides monounsaturated fats.

Promotes heart health

Protein Choices: Chicken provides high-quality protein.

To grow and repair muscles.

Benefits of Stir Fry

Vegetables: A variety of vegetables ensures a high intake of vitamins, minerals, and fiber.

To support immune system.

Aid in digestion.

Ingredients & Tools

For the Stir Fry:

- 2 tablespoons vegetable oil
- 2 chicken breasts, thinly sliced
- 3 cups of mixed vegetables (such as bell peppers, broccoli, carrots, and snap peas)
- 1 onion, sliced
- 2 cloves garlic, minced
- 1 tablespoon fresh ginger, grated

For the Sauce:

- 1/4 cup soy sauce (low sodium)
- 1 tablespoon sesame oil
- 1 tablespoon honey or maple syrup (optional)
- 1 tablespoon cornstarch dissolved in 2 tablespoons water
- Optional: Add chili flakes or hot sauce for heat

Tips for Success

High Heat: Keep the heat high to cook the vegetables quickly while retaining their crunch and nutrients.

Customization: Feel free to swap out any of the vegetables or proteins based on preferences and what you have available. Stir fry is exceptionally adaptable.

Preparation: Having all ingredients prepped and ready to go before you start cooking is crucial since the cooking process is fast.

It is recommended to pair the stir fry with a source of complex carbohydrates like brown rice or whole grain noodles for a balanced meal. Portion control is essential, especially if including higher-calorie sauces or toppings.

METHOD

Step 1: Slice the chicken and vegetables into thin, even pieces to ensure quick and even cooking. Grate the ginger and mince the garlic. In a small bowl, combine soy sauce, sesame oil, honey or maple syrup if using, and the cornstarch-water mixture. Set aside.

Step 2: Heat the oil in a large skillet or wok over high heat.

Add the chicken and stir-fry until it starts to brown, about 3-4 minutes. Add the onions, garlic, and ginger, cooking for another 2 minutes until fragrant.

Add the mixed vegetables and stir-fry until just tender, about 4-5 minutes.

Step 3:

Pour the sauce over the stir-fried ingredients. Mix well to combine and coat everything evenly.

Continue to cook for another 2 minutes until the sauce has thickened.

Step 4:

Serve immediately over rice, noodles, or quinoa.

Garnish with sesame seeds or sliced green onions if desired.

Per Serving:

- Calories: 250-300
- Protein: 20-25g
- Fat: 10-15g
- Carbohydrates: 20-25g
- Fiber: 3-4g
- Sodium: 500-600mg

NOTES

RATING

DIFFICULTY

Meatloaf

PREP 20 MIN | COOK 1 HOUR | 6 SERVES

Benefits of Meatloaf

Lean Ground Beef: Provides high-quality protein and is a good source of iron and B vitamins.

To grow and repair muscles.

For energy production.

Vegetables: A variety of vegetables ensures a high intake of vitamins, minerals, and fiber.

To support immune system.

Whole Wheat Breadcrumbs: Higher in fiber than regular breadcrumbs.

Aid in digestion.

Ingredients & Tools

For the Meatloaf:

- 1 1/2 pounds ground beef (use lean ground beef for a healthier option)
- 1 cup breadcrumbs (use whole wheat breadcrumbs for added fiber)
- 1 onion, finely chopped
- 1 carrot, grated
- 1 celery stalk, finely chopped
- 2 garlic cloves, minced
- 1/2 cup milk (use skim milk to reduce fat)
- 1 egg, beaten
- 2 tablespoons Worcestershire sauce
- 1 teaspoon dried thyme
- Salt and pepper to taste

For the Glaze:

- 1/2 cup ketchup
- 2 tablespoons brown sugar (reduce or substitute with honey for a healthier option)
- 1 tablespoon apple cider vinegar

Tips for Success

Moisture is Key: Ensure the meatloaf doesn't dry out by not overmixing the meat and by adding enough moist ingredients like milk and egg.

Let It Rest: Allowing the meatloaf to rest after baking will help redistribute the juices throughout the meatloaf, making it moist and easier to slice.

It is recommended to be mindful of portion sizes as meatloaf can be quite dense and filling. Serve with a side of steamed vegetables like green beans or carrots and a portion of mashed potatoes for a traditional, balanced meal.

METHOD

Step 1: Preheat your oven to 350°F (175°C). In a large bowl, combine the ground beef, breadcrumbs, onion, carrot, celery, garlic, milk, egg, Worcestershire sauce, thyme, salt, and pepper. Mix well until everything is evenly distributed.

Step 2: Transfer the meat mixture to a loaf pan or shape it into a loaf on a baking sheet lined with parchment paper. In a small bowl, mix together the ketchup, brown sugar, and apple cider vinegar.

Spread half of the glaze evenly over the meatloaf.

Step 3: Place the meatloaf in the oven and bake for 45 minutes. After 45 minutes, spread the remaining glaze over the meatloaf and continue to bake for another 15 minutes, or until the meatloaf is cooked through and reaches an internal temperature of 160°F (71°C).

Step 4: Let the meatloaf rest for 10 minutes before slicing. This helps retain the juices and makes slicing easier. Serve warm.

Per Serving:

- Calories: 350-400
- Protein: 25-30g
- Fat: 15-20g
- Carbohydrates: 20-25g
- Fiber: 2-3g
- Sodium: 500-600mg

NOTES

RATING

DIFFICULTY

Baked Ham

PREP 20 MIN

COOK 2.5 HOUR

12 SERVES

Benefits of Baked Ham

Ham: Provides high-quality protein and essential nutrients, including iron, zinc, and B vitamins.

To grow and repair muscles.

For energy production.

Pineapple Juice: Contains vitamin C and manganese, which are antioxidants

To support immune system.

For strong bones and teeth.

Cinnamon: Offers anti-inflammatory properties.

Can help regulate blood sugar levels.

Ingredients & Tools

For the Ham:

- 1 whole bone-in ham (about 8-10 pounds)
- Whole cloves (optional, for studding the ham)

For the Glaze:

- 1/2 cup brown sugar (use less or substitute with honey)
- 1/4 cup Dijon mustard
- 1/4 cup apple cider vinegar
- 1/4 cup pineapple juice (or orange juice)
- 1 tablespoon ground cinnamon

Tips for Success

Basting Frequently: Regular basting with the glaze helps to keep the ham moist and adds flavor to every slice.

Cloves for Added Flavor: Studding the ham with cloves can impart a subtle spiciness that complements the sweetness of the glaze.

It is recommended to be aware of portion sizes, especially given the higher sodium content in ham. Complementing the meal with low-sodium and fiber-rich sides can help balance nutrition.

METHOD

Step 1: Preheat your oven to 325°F (165°C). If your ham is not pre-sliced, score the surface of the ham in a diamond pattern and stud with cloves if desired. Place the ham in a roasting pan, flat side down.

Step 2: Make the Glaze:
In a small saucepan over low heat, combine brown sugar, Dijon mustard, apple cider vinegar, pineapple juice, and cinnamon. Heat the mixture, stirring until the sugar is dissolved and the glaze is smooth.

Step 3: Bake the Ham:
Brush the ham with about a third of the glaze. Cover the ham loosely with aluminum foil to prevent drying out. Bake in the preheated oven for 2 hours, basting every 30 minutes with the additional glaze.

Step 4: Final Glazing and Serving:
After 2 hours, remove the foil and increase the oven temperature to 400°F (200°C). Apply the remaining glaze and bake for an additional 30 minutes, or until the surface is caramelized and golden. Remove from the oven and let rest for 10-15 minutes before slicing.

Per Serving:

- Calories: 350-400
- Protein: 25-30g
- Fat: 20-25g
- Carbohydrates: 15-20g
- Sodium: 1000-1100mg
- Sugar: 9 g

NOTES

RATING

DIFFICULTY

Desserts
Brownies

PREP 15 MIN

COOK 20-25 MIN

12 SERVES

Benefits of Brownies

Cocoa Powder: Rich in polyphenols, which are antioxidants that help reduce inflammation.

To improve blood flow.

To enhance brain function and mood.

Nuts: If added, nuts provide healthy fats, proteins, fiber, and various vitamins and minerals.

To support immune system.

Whole Wheat or Almond Flour: These flours offer more fiber and nutrients compared to all-purpose flour.

To provide a slower release of energy.

Ingredients & Tools

For the Brownies:

- 1/2 cup unsalted butter (or substitute with coconut oil for a healthier option)
- 1 cup granulated sugar (reduce amount or substitute with a natural sweetener like coconut sugar)
- 2 large eggs
- 1 teaspoon vanilla extract
- 1/3 cup unsweetened cocoa powder
- 1/2 cup all-purpose flour (use whole wheat flour or almond flour for a healthier alternative)
- 1/4 teaspoon salt
- 1/4 teaspoon baking powder

Optional Add-ins:

- 1/2 cup chopped walnuts or pecans (optional, for added texture and nutrients)
- 1/2 cup dark chocolate chips (optional)

Tips for Success

Don't Overmix: Mix the ingredients until just combined to keep the brownies dense and fudgy.

Check Doneness: Use a toothpick inserted in the center to check for doneness – it should come out with a few moist crumbs.

Cool Completely: Allow the brownies to cool completely in the pan for clean cuts.

It is recommended to enjoy brownies as an occasional treat and be mindful of portion sizes. Pair a small brownie with a serving of fruit or a dairy product like Greek yogurt.

METHOD

Step 1: Preheat your oven to 350°F (175°C). Grease a 9x9 inch baking pan or line it with parchment paper.

Step 2: In a medium saucepan, melt the butter over low heat. Remove from heat and stir in sugar, eggs, and vanilla. Beat in cocoa, flour, salt, and baking powder. Spread the batter into the prepared pan.

If using, sprinkle chopped nuts and chocolate chips over the top.

Step 3: Bake in preheated oven for 20 to 25 minutes. Do not overcook; the brownies should be soft in the center.

Step 4: Let the brownies cool in the pan before slicing into squares. Serve as is, or with a scoop of vanilla ice cream for an indulgent treat.

Per Serving:

- Calories: 180-200
- Protein: 2-3g
- Fat: 10-12g
- Carbohydrates: 22-25g
- Fiber: 1-2g
- Sodium: 50-60mg

NOTES

RATING

DIFFICULTY

Ice Cream Sundae

PREP 5 MIN

COOK 0 MIN

1 SERVE

Benefits of Ice Cream Sundae

Ice cream is a dairy product, so it naturally contains calcium and phosphorus.

For strong bones and teeth.

Nuts: If added, nuts provide healthy fats, proteins, fiber, and various vitamins and minerals.

To support immune system.

Fresh Fruit: Provides essential vitamins, minerals, and dietary fiber.

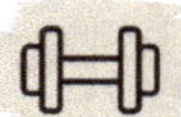

to stay fit and healthy.

Aid in digestion.

Ingredients & Tools

For the Base:

- 2 scoops of your favorite ice cream (choose a lower-fat or dairy-free option for a healthier alternative)
- 1/2 cup fresh fruit (such as sliced strawberries, bananas, or blueberries)

For the Toppings:

- 2 tablespoons chocolate syrup (use a sugar-free version if preferred)
- 1 tablespoon crushed nuts (almonds, walnuts, or pecans for added crunch and nutrients)
- Whipped cream (opt for light whipped cream or a coconut-based alternative for fewer calories)
- 1 cherry for the top

Tips for Success

Chill the Sundae Glass: For a special touch, chill the sundae glass in the freezer before assembling to help keep the ice cream from melting too quickly.

Varied Textures: Include ingredients with different textures to make each bite interesting—from creamy and soft to crunchy and crisp.

It is recommended to enjoy ice cream sundae as an occasional treat rather than a regular part of your diet.

METHOD

Step 1: Prepare the Ice Cream:
Scoop your chosen ice cream into a serving bowl or sundae glass.

Step 2: Add Fresh Fruit:
Layer the sliced or chopped fresh fruit on top of the ice cream.

Step 3: Add Toppings:
Drizzle the chocolate syrup over the ice cream and fruit.
Sprinkle the crushed nuts for a crunchy texture.

Step 4: Add a dollop of whipped cream on top. Place a cherry on the peak of the whipped cream as a classic garnish.

Per Serving:

- Calories: 250-300
- Protein: 3-5g
- Fat: 15-20g
- Carbohydrates: 25-35g
- Fiber: 2-3g
- Sodium: 50-100mg

NOTES

RATING

DIFFICULTY

Cupcakes

PREP 20 MIN

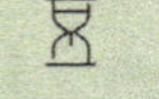

COOK 20 MIN

12 SERVES

Benefits of Cupcakes

Milk in cupcakes is a source of calcium

For strong bones and teeth.

Whole Wheat Flour: Offers more fiber and nutrients than all-purpose flour.

To provide a slower release of energy.

Almond Milk: A good alternative for those who are lactose intolerant, providing vitamins like vitamin E without the saturated fats found in cow's milk.

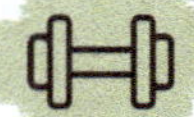

to stay fit and healthy

Natural Sweeteners: Options like honey or maple syrup can offer minerals and antioxidants

To support immune system

Ingredients & Tools

For the Cupcakes:

- 1 1/2 cups all-purpose flour (use whole wheat or almond flour for a healthier option)
- 1 teaspoon baking powder
- 1/2 teaspoon salt
- 1/2 cup unsalted butter, softened (use coconut oil or applesauce for a lower fat option)
- 1 cup granulated sugar (or substitute like honey or maple syrup)
- 2 large eggs
- 2 teaspoons vanilla extract
- 1/2 cup milk (use almond or oat milk for a dairy-free option)

For the Frosting:

- 1/2 cup unsalted butter, softened (use vegan butter for a dairy-free option)
- 2 cups powdered sugar (use less)
- 2 tablespoons milk (use a non-dairy milk if preferred)
- 1 teaspoon vanilla extract

Tips for Success

Do Not Overmix: When combining wet and dry ingredients, mix until just combined to avoid dense cupcakes.

Cool Completely Before Frosting: Ensure cupcakes are at room temperature before applying frosting to prevent them from melting.

It is recommended that you enjoy cupcakes as a treat with a balanced diet. Given the sugar and fat content, consider smaller or mini cupcakes if serving to children or at large gatherings to control portion sizes.

METHOD

Step 1: Preheat your oven to 350°F (175°C). Line a muffin tin with cupcake liners. In a bowl, sift together the flour, baking powder, and salt. Set aside.

Step 2: In a large mixing bowl, cream the softened butter and sugar until light and fluffy.
Beat in the eggs one at a time, then stir in the vanilla extract.
Alternately add the dry ingredients and milk to the butter mixture, starting and ending with the dry ingredients. Mix until just combined.

Step 3: Spoon the batter into the cupcake liners, filling each about two-thirds full. Bake for 18-20 minutes, or until a toothpick inserted into the center comes out clean. Remove from the oven and allow to cool in the pan for 5 minutes, then transfer to a wire rack to cool completely.

Step 4: In a mixing bowl, beat the softened butter until creamy.
Gradually beat in powdered sugar, then mix in the milk and vanilla until smooth and spreadable. Once the cupcakes are completely cool, frost them using a knife or piping bag.

Per Serving:

- Calories: 250-300
- Protein: 3-4g
- Fat: 12-15g
- Carbohydrates: 35-40g
- Fiber: 1-2g
- Sodium: 150-200mg

NOTES

RATING

DIFFICULTY

Chocolate Chip Cookies

PREP 15 MIN

COOK 10 MIN (per batch)

36 SERVES

Benefits of Chocolate Chip Cookies

Dark Chocolate Chips: Contain antioxidants, particularly flavanols.

To improve blood flow.

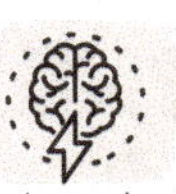

To enhance brain function and mood.

Nuts: If added, nuts provide healthy fats, proteins, fiber, and various vitamins and minerals.

To support immune system.

Whole Wheat Flour: Offers more fiber and nutrients than all-purpose flour.

To provide a slower release of energy.

Ingredients & Tools

For the Cookies:

- 1 cup (2 sticks) unsalted butter, softened (or substitute with coconut oil for a healthier option)
- 3/4 cup granulated sugar
- 3/4 cup brown sugar, packed (reduce to 1/2 cup for less sweetness or use a natural sweetener)
- 2 large eggs
- 2 teaspoons vanilla extract
- 2 1/4 cups all-purpose flour (substitute half with whole wheat flour for added fiber)
- 1 teaspoon baking soda
- 1/2 teaspoon salt
- 2 cups semisweet chocolate chips (use dark chocolate chips for less sugar and more antioxidants)
- Optional: 1 cup chopped nuts (such as walnuts or pecans)

Tips for Success

Don't Overbake: For softer cookies, pull them out of the oven when they are just set and still look a bit underdone in the middle.

Cooling: Letting cookies cool on the pan for a few minutes helps them set without becoming too hard.

It is recommended to enjoy these cookies in moderation as an occasional treat within a balanced diet. Serve with a glass of milk or a cup of tea for a comforting snack.

METHOD

Step 1: Preheat your oven to 375°F (190°C). Line baking sheets with parchment paper or silicone baking mats.

Step 2: In a large mixing bowl, cream together the softened butter, granulated sugar, and brown sugar until smooth and fluffy. Beat in the eggs one at a time, then stir in the vanilla.

Step 3: In another bowl, whisk together the flour, baking soda, and salt. Gradually beat the dry ingredients into the butter mixture until just blended. Stir in the chocolate chips and nuts, if using, until evenly distributed.

Step 4: Drop rounded tablespoons of the dough onto the prepared baking sheets, spaced about 2 inches apart. Bake in the preheated oven for 9 to 11 minutes, or until the edges are golden. Allow the cookies to cool on the baking sheet for 5 minutes before transferring to a wire rack to cool completely.

Per Serving:

- Calories: 160-180
- Protein: 2g
- Fat: 9-10g
- Carbohydrates: 18-20g
- Fiber: 1g
- Sodium: 85mg

NOTES

RATING

DIFFICULTY

Apple Pie

PREP 30 MIN

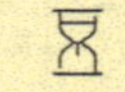
COOK 50 MIN

8 SERVES

Benefits of Apple Pie

Apples: Rich in dietary fiber, vitamin C, and various antioxidants.

To support immune system.

Promotes heart health.

Cinnamon and Nutmeg: Both spices are known for their anti-inflammatory properties.

Can help regulate blood sugar levels.

Whole Wheat Flour: Provides additional fiber and nutrients compared to all-purpose flour.

Aid in digestion.

Ingredients & Tools

For the Crust:

- 2 1/2 cups all-purpose flour (substitute half with whole wheat flour for added nutrients)
- 1 teaspoon salt
- 1 teaspoon sugar (optional)
- 1 cup unsalted butter, chilled and diced
- 1/4 to 1/2 cup ice water

For the Filling:

6 cups thinly sliced and peeled apples

- 3/4 cup sugar (reduce to 1/2 cup or use a natural sweetener like honey for a healthier option)
- 2 tablespoons all-purpose flour
- 1 teaspoon ground cinnamon
- 1/4 teaspoon ground nutmeg
- 1/2 teaspoon lemon zest
- 1 tablespoon lemon juice
- 1 tablespoon butter, to dot
- 1 egg yolk, beaten with 1 tablespoon water

Tips for Success

Apple Selection: Using a mix of different types of apples can enhance the flavor and texture of the pie.

Chilling the Dough: Ensure the dough is well-chilled to make it easier to work with and to help prevent shrinkage during baking.

It is recommended to enjoy apple pie in moderation, given the sugar and fat content. Complement the pie with a scoop of low-fat vanilla ice cream or a dollop of whipped cream for added delight.

METHOD

Step 1: Prepare the Crust:

In a large bowl, combine flour, salt, and sugar. Add the chilled, diced butter and mix until the mixture resembles coarse crumbs.

Gradually add ice water, stirring until the mixture forms a ball. Wrap in plastic and refrigerate for at least 30 minutes.

Step 2: Make the Filling:

In a large bowl, toss the sliced apples with sugar, flour, cinnamon, nutmeg, lemon zest, and lemon juice. Set aside.

Step 3: Preheat your oven to 375°F (190°C). Roll out half of the dough to fit a 9-inch pie plate. Place crust in pie plate. Fill with apple mixture and dot with butter. Roll out the second half of the dough to cover the top. Trim, seal, and flute the edges. Cut slits in the top to allow steam to escape.

Step 4: Brush with the egg wash for a golden finish. Bake in the preheated oven for 50 minutes, or until the crust is golden brown and the filling is bubbly. If the edges brown too quickly, cover them with foil. Let the pie cool on a wire rack before serving to allow the filling to set.

Per Serving:

- Calories: 400-450
- Protein: 3-5g
- Fat: 20-25g
- Carbohydrates: 50-60g
- Fiber: 3-4g
- Sodium: 300-400mg

NOTES

RATING

DIFFICULTY

Cheesecake

PREP 30 MIN

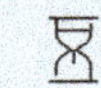
COOK 50 MIN

8 SERVES

Benefits of Cheesecake

Cream Cheese and Sour Cream: Both provide a good amount of calcium and protein.

For strong bones and teeth.

Eggs: High in protein and contain essential amino acids, vitamins, and minerals.

To grow and repair muscles.

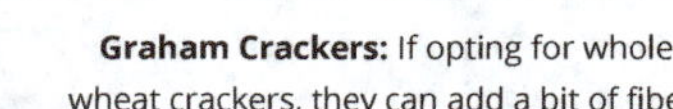

Graham Crackers: If opting for whole wheat crackers, they can add a bit of fiber.

Aid in digestion.

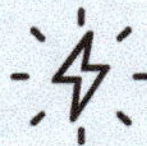

To provide a slower release of energy.

Ingredients & Tools

For the Crust:

- 1 1/2 cups graham cracker crumbs (use whole wheat crackers for a healthier option)
- 1/3 cup unsalted butter, melted (substitute with coconut oil for a healthier version)
- 1/4 cup sugar (reduce or substitute with a natural sweetener like honey)

Optional Toppings:

- Fresh berries, fruit compote, or homemade caramel sauce

For the Filling:

- 4 (8 ounce) packages cream cheese, softened (use low-fat cream cheese for fewer calories)
- 1 cup sugar (reduce to 3/4 cup or use a natural sweetener like honey)
- 1 teaspoon vanilla extract
- 4 large eggs
- 2 tablespoons all-purpose flour (optional, helps stabilize the filling)
- 1/2 cup sour cream (use low-fat sour cream or Greek yogurt)

Tips for Success

Water Bath: To avoid cracks, bake the cheesecake in a water bath. This helps maintain a gentle and even heat around the cheesecake.

Cooling Gradually: Allow the cheesecake to cool gradually in the turned-off oven to minimize the risk of cracking.

It is recommended to consume cheesecake in moderation, given its richness in fats and sugars. Pair a small serving of cheesecake with a light meal that includes plenty of fruits.

METHOD

Step 1: Prepare the Crust:

Mix graham cracker crumbs, melted butter, and sugar in a bowl until well combined. Press the mixture into the bottom of a 9-inch springform pan, forming a tight and even layer. Chill in the refrigerator while preparing the filling.

Step 2: Make the Filling:

In a large mixing bowl, beat the cream cheese with sugar and vanilla extract until smooth and creamy.

Add eggs one at a time, fully incorporating after each addition. Avoid over-mixing.

Stir in flour and sour cream until just combined.

Step 3: Assemble and Bake:

Preheat your oven to 325°F (163°C).

Pour the filling over the prepared crust and smooth the top with a spatula.

Bake in the preheated oven for about 55-60 minutes. The center should be set, but slightly wobbly.

Step 4: Turn off the oven, slightly open the oven door, and let the cheesecake cool in the oven for 1 hour to prevent cracks.After cooling, refrigerate the cheesecake for at least 3 hours, preferably overnight. Remove the cheesecake from the springform pan, slice, and serve with your choice of toppings like fresh berries or a fruit compote.

Per Serving:

- Calories: 450-500
- Protein: 8-10g
- Fat: 30-35g
- Carbohydrates: 40-45g
- Fiber: 1-2g
- Sodium: 350-400mg

NOTES

RATING

DIFFICULTY

Chocolate Cake

PREP 30 MIN
(1 hour cooling)

COOK 30-35 MIN

12 SERVES

Benefits of Chocolate Cake

Cocoa Powder: Rich in polyphenols, which are antioxidants that help reduce inflammation.

To improve blood flow.

To enhance brain function and mood.

Alternative Milks: Non-dairy milks often contain added vitamins and minerals.

To support immune system.

Whole Wheat flour: Offers more fiber and nutrients compared to all-purpose flour.

To provide a slower release of energy.

Ingredients & Tools

For the Cake:

- 1 3/4 cups all-purpose flour (substitute half with whole wheat flour)
- 2 cups sugar (use a natural sweetener like coconut sugar)
- 3/4 cup unsweetened cocoa powder (use dark cocoa powder)
- 1 1/2 teaspoons baking powder
- 1 1/2 teaspoons baking soda
- 1 teaspoon salt
- 2 large eggs
- 1 cup whole milk (use almond or oat milk for a dairy-free option)
- 1/2 cup vegetable oil (or substitute with applesauce for less fat)
- 2 teaspoons vanilla extract
- 1 cup boiling water

For the Frosting:

- 3/4 cup butter, softened (use plant-based butter for a vegan version)
- 2/3 cup unsweetened cocoa powder
- 3 cups powdered sugar (reduce to 2 cups for less sweetness)
- 1/3 cup milk (or a non-dairy milk alternative)
- 1 teaspoon vanilla extract

Tips for Success

Cake Texture: For a moist cake, don't overbake. Start checking the cake 5-10 minutes before the expected finish time.

Cooling: Ensure the cake layers are completely cool before frosting to prevent the frosting from melting.

It is recommended to enjoy chocolate cake in moderation, given its richness. The cake is perfect for birthdays, celebrations, or any special occasion where a decadent treat is called for.

METHOD

Step 1: Prepare the Oven and Pans:

Preheat your oven to 350°F (175°C). Grease and flour two 9-inch round cake pans.

Step 2: Mix Dry Ingredients:

In a large bowl, stir together flour, sugar, cocoa, baking powder, baking soda, and salt. Add eggs, milk, oil, and vanilla to the flour mixture and mix until well combined. Carefully stir in boiling water (the batter will be thin).

Step 3: Bake the Cake:

Pour batter into prepared pans.

Bake for 30 to 35 minutes in the preheated oven, until a toothpick inserted into the center comes out clean.

Allow to cool in the pans for 10 minutes, then remove to wire racks to cool completely.

Step 4: Make the Frosting:

In a medium bowl, combine softened butter, cocoa powder, powdered sugar, milk, and vanilla extract. Beat until smooth and fluffy. Once the cakes are completely cool, frost the top of one cake layer, then place the second layer on top and continue frosting the top and sides of the cake.

Per Serving:

- Calories: 350-400
- Protein: 5-6g
- Fat: 15-20g
- Carbohydrates: 50-55g
- Fiber: 3-4g
- Sodium: 300-400mg

NOTES

RATING

DIFFICULTY

Donuts

PREP 2 HOURS (including rising)

COOK 30 MIN

12 SERVES

Benefits of Donuts

Eggs: Contain high-quality protein and important vitamins and minerals

To grow and repair muscles.

To support immune system.

Milk: Provides calcium

For strong bones and teeth.

Whole Wheat flour: Offers more fiber and nutrients compared to all-purpose flour

To provide a slower release of energy.

Ingredients & Tools

For the Dough:

- 2 1/4 teaspoons active dry yeast (1 packet)
- 2/3 cup warm milk (about 110°F, use almond or oat milk for a dairy-free option)
- 1/4 cup granulated sugar (reduce or use a natural sweetener like honey)
- 1/2 teaspoon salt
- 1/4 cup unsalted butter, melted (substitute with coconut oil)
- 2 large eggs
- 4 cups all-purpose flour (substitute half with whole wheat flour for added fiber)
- Vegetable oil for frying (use a healthier option like canola or sunflower oil)

For the Glaze:

- 1/2 cup powdered sugar (reduce to 1/3 cup for less sweetness)
- 1 tablespoon milk (or non-dairy milk)
- 1/2 teaspoon vanilla extract

Tips for Success

Consistent Temperature: Ensure the oil remains at a steady temperature for even frying.

Handling Dough: Handle the dough as little as possible after rising to keep the donuts light and airy.

It is recommended to enjoy donuts as an occasional treat, due to their high sugar and fat content. If enjoying donuts in the morning, pair with a protein-rich food like Greek yogurt or a handful of nuts to balance the meal.

METHOD

Step 1: In a large bowl, dissolve the yeast in warm milk. Add sugar, salt, melted butter, eggs, and 2 cups of flour. Beat until smooth. Mix in enough remaining flour to form a soft dough (it should be slightly sticky but manageable). Place the dough in a greased bowl, turning once to grease the top. Cover and let rise in a warm place until doubled, about 1 hour.

Step 2: Punch down the dough and turn onto a floured surface. Roll out to 1/2 inch thickness. Cut with a floured donut cutter or use a large cookie cutter for shapes and a smaller cutter for holes.Place donuts on a floured baking sheet. Cover and let rise until doubled, about 30 minutes.

Step 3: Heat oil in a deep fryer or large pan to 375°F (190°C).

Fry donuts, a few at a time, until golden brown on both sides, about 1 minute per side.

Remove from the oil and drain on paper towels.

Step 4: In a small bowl, mix powdered sugar, milk, and vanilla until smooth.

Dip each donut into the glaze while still warm, then set on a wire rack to drip off excess and cool.

Per Serving:

- Calories: 250-300
- Protein: 4-5g
- Fat: 10-12g
- Carbohydrates: 35-40g
- Fiber: 1-2g
- Sodium: 100-150mg

NOTES

RATING

DIFFICULTY

Rice Krispies Treats

PREP 10 MIN
(Cooling Time: 30 minutes)

COOK 10 MIN

12 SERVES

Benefits of Rice Krispies Treats

Coconut Oil: contains a significant amount of lauric acid, which can have antimicrobial and antifungal effects.

To support immune system.

Marshmallows: Mainly provide sugar, offering quick energy, though they're low in nutrients.

Quick source of energy.

Rice Krispies: Provide some iron and vitamins when fortified, but are primarily a source of quick-digesting carbohydrates.

Aid in digestion.

For strong bones and teeth.

Ingredients & Tools

- 3 tablespoons unsalted butter (substitute with coconut oil for a vegan option)
- 1 package (about 10 oz, or approximately 40) marshmallows (use vegan marshmallows if needed)
- 6 cups Rice Krispies cereal (or any puffed rice cereal)

Tips for Success

Even Coating: To ensure every piece of cereal gets coated with the marshmallow mixture, add the cereal in increments and mix thoroughly each time.

Prevent Sticking: Keep your hands or the spatula greased with butter or cooking spray to prevent sticking when pressing the mixture into the pan.

It is recommended to enjoy these treats as an occasional treat, due to their high sugar content. Pair a Rice Krispies Treat with a source of protein or healthy fat, like nuts or a piece of cheese, to balance the intake of sugars and carbohydrates.

METHOD

Step 1: Melt the Butter:
In a large saucepan over low heat, melt the butter. This can also be done in a microwave-safe bowl in the microwave.

Step 2: Add Marshmallows:
Add marshmallows to the melted butter. Stir until completely melted and the mixture is smooth. If using a microwave, return the bowl to the microwave and heat for 30 seconds at a time, stirring in between, until marshmallows are fully melted.

Step 3: Mix in the Cereal:
Remove from heat (or take out of the microwave) and immediately add the Rice Krispies cereal. Stir until the cereal is well coated with the marshmallow mixture.

Step 4: Press into Pan:
Using a buttered spatula or wax paper, evenly press the mixture into a 13 x 9 x 2-inch pan coated with cooking spray. Make sure the surface is even. Cool and Cut:
Let the treats cool completely at room temperature for about 30 minutes. Cut into 12 squares.

Per Serving:

- Calories: 150-160
- Protein: 1-2g
- Fat: 3-4g
- Carbohydrates: 29-31g
- Fiber: 0g
- Sodium: 70-90mg

NOTES

RATING

DIFFICULTY

Banana Split

PREP 10 MIN

COOK 0 MIN

1 SERVE

Benefits of Banana Split

Bananas: Provide potassium, vitamin C, vitamin B6, and fiber.

For heart health.

Low-Fat or Non-Dairy Ice Cream: Reduces intake of saturated fats and is suitable for those with lactose intolerance.

Aid in digestion.

Berries and Pineapple: Offer vitamins, antioxidants, and fiber.

To support immune system.

Nuts: Contain healthy fats, protein, and fiber.

To provide satiety.

Ingredients & Tools

- 1 large banana
- 1 scoop each of vanilla, chocolate, and strawberry ice cream (use low-fat or non-dairy alternatives for a healthier option)
- 2 tablespoons pineapple chunks (fresh or canned in juice)
- 2 tablespoons strawberry slices
- 2 tablespoons whipped cream (use a low-fat version or a coconut-based alternative)
- 1 tablespoon chopped nuts (such as almonds, walnuts, or pecans)
- 1 tablespoon chocolate syrup (use a sugar-free version if preferred)
- 1 maraschino cherry

Tips for Success

Banana Quality: Use a ripe but firm banana, which will hold up better when split and filled.

Serving Immediately: Serve the banana split immediately after assembling to prevent the ice cream from melting and the banana from browning.

It is recommended to enjoy banana split as an occasional treat due to its high sugar and calorie content. If having a banana split, consider lighter meals throughout the day to balance your overall calorie and sugar intake.

METHOD

Step 1: Prepare the Banana:
Peel the banana and split it lengthwise. Place the two halves in a long, shallow dish, side by side with the inside facing up.

Step 2: Add Ice Cream:
Scoop one ball each of vanilla, chocolate, and strawberry ice cream and arrange them in a line between the banana slices.

Step 3: Add Toppings:
Sprinkle the pineapple chunks (optionally) and strawberry slices over the ice cream. Drizzle chocolate syrup over the top.

Step 4: Add a dollop of whipped cream on each scoop of ice cream. Sprinkle with chopped nuts. Top with a maraschino cherry.

Per Serving:

- Calories: 500-550
- Protein: 8-10g
- Fat: 25-30g
- Carbohydrates: 65-70g
- Fiber: 4-5g
- Sodium: 100-150mg

NOTES

RATING

DIFFICULTY

Thank you for going on this culinary adventure!

I hope you had as much fun discovering the recipes in this cookbook as I did making them for you. If you loved your experience, please consider leaving an **Amazon review**. Your comment helps me on my journey as a new author and helps other young chefs discover and trust this cookbook. And while you're there, remember to look at my other products developed specifically for teens. There's plenty more to uncover!

Adulting Life Skills For Teen Boys Over 101 Key Abilities for Success in Communication, Problem-Solving and Self-Discipline.

The book offers a guide for teenage boys, teaching them to navigate life's challenges with confidence, resilience, and practical skills. Through engaging stories of three relatable characters—Mike, Alex, and Joe—this book provides a dynamic blend of actionable strategies, essential life skills, and personal growth lessons, making it an indispensable resource for any teen boy's journey into adulthood.

Crafting Books that Inspire Confidence and Help Develop Essential Life Skills!